Unrestrained

Surviving and Thriving After Abuse

Caroline Cameron

GRACE
PUBLISHING
Dyslexic Friendly

Copyright © 2020 Caroline Cameron

23 22 21 20 19 7 6 5 4 3 2 1

First published 2020 by Sarah Grace Publishing,
an imprint of Malcolm Down Publishing Ltd.
www.malcolmdown.co.uk

The right of Caroline Cameron to be identified as the author
of this work has been asserted by her in accordance with the
Copyright, Designs and Patents Act 1988.

British Library Cataloguing in Publication Data
A catalogue record for this book is available from the British Library.

ISBN 978-1-912863-44-0

Cover design by Anton Fowler, Bubble Design.

Printed in the UK

What Others Are Saying

It's been said that the key to writing is to sit down, take a pen and open a vein. In this moving, poignant book, Caroline does just that. But this is a story of redemption and hope, of the light of God that overcomes the deepest darkness. This book will empower any who have been scarred by abuse, and resource any who seek to help the abused in a journey of recovery. Vital, powerful, and highly recommended.

Jeff Lucas, author, speaker, broadcaster.

I didn't have time to read this book. I had offered to write an endorsement and thought reading the first chapter would give me ideas. Wow! I couldn't put it down! I read the entire book in one sitting. You have in your hands an incredible story written with courage and intense authenticity by a wonderfully humble and faithful follower of Jesus. These pages will be like gold for anyone who is suffering abuse, has suffered from it or loves and cares for anyone who has. It is an incredible treasure trove of wisdom and hope and I know that it is going to have a powerful kingdom impact wherever it goes. You will be moved, you will be changed, you will be inspired as you read this book.

Simon Holley, Senior Leader of King's Arms Church, Bedford and Team Leader of Catalyst Network, Newfrontiers.

Caroline worked alongside me for a number of years in Lincoln. Though I knew something of her journey, I could never have appreciated the depth and pain of her story of abuse. Her levels of commitment and service, combined with her communication and people skills, pointed to a healthy, seasoned church leader. This courageous and transparent account of her battles focuses on a Saviour who not only forgives sins, but brings freedom, healing and restoration. I can personally testify that Caroline is truly an over-comer who is a walking example of God's healing power and grace.

Stuart Bell, Senior Pastor of Alive UK and Leader of Ground Level Network.

Caroline Cameron has produced a moving and challenging book. Her honesty and openness is outstanding. It's raw, real and lifts the mask off so much of the secret and dangerous world of domestic abuse and so much more. It's a must read for anyone who cares about violence and injustice against women.

Michele Hawthorne, Founder of Press Red.

This book is a life-changer! It is a sometimes frightening, often staggering story of one woman's journey into, through and out of the most horrific abuse, but, more importantly, into healing and restoration of soul. Caroline has achieved an amazing thing in writing it – she has bared her soul, told a heart-wrenching story, married those things with the rich learnings derived from her relationship with God her heavenly Father, and served them as a rich feast of practical Grace for any hungry reader.

Stories like this one can sometimes break our hearts, but not put them together again. Or they can "heal the wounds of my people lightly" with clichés or pat answers. Caroline, however, has not left us in either of those places, but has rather approached her story with the searing honesty and no-nonsense practicality which I have seen in her from the day we met. And in doing that, she has dug a well of healing for the thousands of people whose stories are like hers. She has

marked a way in this particular wilderness and made the valley of Achor a doorway of hope.
Costa Mitchell, National Director Emeritus, Vineyard Churches, South Africa.

Caroline writes boldly, bravely and with great clarity about a personal journey from terrifying abuse and all that comes in its wake to a place of true freedom. The sensitive and often unstated issues surrounding abuse are exposed, along with a clear pathway towards hope and freedom. I highly recommend this book to you and encourage you to apply the lessons within and walk, as Caroline did, your journey to freedom with God as your Father.
Paul Benger, Senior Pastor of Ikon Church.

Caroline writes with transparency, vulnerability and great courage. She offers hope and wisdom for those caught in destructive and abusive relationships, as well as those who want to help others find freedom. An uncomfortable read that demonstrates the power of faith over fear.
Steve and Angie Campbell, Senior Pastors of The C3 Church, UK.

We knew Caroline Cameron as a confident and competent leader while we lived in the UK. She hosted us at her table with lively meals and enjoyable conversation as we served in the same church together. We experienced Caroline as she "thrived", but until reading *Unrestrained: Surviving and Thriving After Abuse,* we had no idea all she had suffered and survived. This is a raw and riveting account of a real-life struggle with physical, sexual and emotional abuse. As pastors, we are excited about having this resource to offer hope and first-hand comfort to those who have also experienced abuse.

Her story will reach hearts in a way no sermon can. We believe the truth plainly presented could be the lifeline to rescue many out of bondage and despair. The "Pause and Reflect" sections at the end of each chapter offer exercises to lead the reader into greater healing and understanding of the truth. This is the season for Caroline to share her powerful story and it will inspire readers to trust God's faithfulness to find you in the middle of every dysfunction and lead you step-by-step into His restoring love and freedom.

Duane and Kris White, Pastors of The Bridge Church, Denton, Texas, USA and Leaders of Beyond These Shores Missions Network.

It is raw, it is real and it is happening to someone right now somewhere as I write. The evil oppression and abuse by one person of another is happening and sometimes, unbeknown to you, to someone you know. Caroline courageously exposes the intimate details of her life to help others escape from living in circumstances that were never designed by God for them. Her story will give you the courage to break free from fear and begin to live again as God intended. Caroline's dependence upon God throughout her life, even in her dark days, is a testimony to her faith and love for God.

Gerrit Di Somma, Founder and Bishop of Carmel Global Ministries Inc USA and Carmel Ministries International UK.

Caroline is a vivacious, fun-loving person! In this honest story, Caroline allows you to walk a journey of Hope with her and learn how to do life well even if it has been challenging. Engaging, practical, healing and empowering – this book will enable you to walk your path of freedom and live life UNRESTRAINED!

Rachel Hickson, Heartcry for Change, Oxford.

Dedication

To my friend, prayer partner and spiritual mother,
Leah Coetzee. You are a gift of God to me.

When you pass through the waters, I will be with you; and when you pass through the rivers, they will not sweep over you. When you walk through the fire, you will not be burned; the flames will not set you ablaze.

(Isaiah 43:2)

Contents

Acknowledgements

I am grateful that I have so many people to thank for this was not a solitary exercise.

I am grateful to my husband, Slim, and my son, Luke. Both are creative people in their own right and see the world from a different vantage point to my own. Slim, thank you for bearing with me as I talked and thought this book through, often preoccupied. Luke, thank you for keeping me grounded in authenticity and honesty when I wanted you to airbrush the wrinkles and lines out of my bio-photo – I love your commitment to choosing the higher and better way!

To my four older children, I am deeply appreciative of the permission you gave me to write this book. I know this came from a place of love and honour for me.

Mum, thank you for the person you are today – full of compassion, faith and heaven bound. I love you so much and have learnt much from you in everyday ways. Thank you for allowing me to tell my childhood story from my perspective. You too are a trophy of Father God's grace and enduring love for us.

Martin, without your strong, direct prophetic prompt at just the right time, I would never have completed this book. Keep listening to the Holy Spirit and bringing those sometimes uncomfortable words. And yes, in answer to a recent prompt, there may be a few more books.

Wendy, Marco and the TSM leadership team, I would not have been courageous enough to write this book without all you have sown into my life while on the course and as a part of its leadership team myself. I am so grateful for your encouragement to be all that God has called me to be and also to keep pursuing the last two percent.

Simon, thank you for your support and exuberant endorsement of this book. Slim and I love the Kings Arms Church. Thank you for modelling authenticity, vulnerability and generosity so well.

Stuart, I am indebted to you for your ongoing support, care and encouragement. You and Irene are part of my journey and I count you as a dear friend.

Gerri, thank you for unselfishly and sacrificially taking me through months of counselling at the beginning of my journey into freedom. I will always remember your kindness. One instance of this is etched on my mind – at a time when I had no money, had lost a lot of weight and was rather pale and lacklustre, you put money into my hand and encouraged me to buy some multi-vitamins. Not something every counsellor would do.

Costa, you are a man of immense wisdom and insight. Thank you for walking with Slim and I as we navigated our way through courtship and into marriage. Without your wise input while I was working through surfacing emotions we would not have made it.

John, thank you for carefully and thoughtfully proofreading the manuscript. Your input was invaluable and you were easy to work with (always an important quality, I feel).

Malcolm and the team at Malcolm Down and Sarah Grace Publishing, many thanks for making the publishing of this first book a delight.

To all those many friends who have been part of my journey, I am so grateful for your input, love, care and support.

My heart overflows with gratitude and love to Father God for holding onto me as I journeyed along an often treacherous path to the place where my experiences of increasing freedom may now help others.

Thank you for reading this book. Thank you for letting go of those things that restrain you and thank you for embracing every ounce of freedom that our loving Father God has for you!

Foreword

Every so often you hear a person's story and it leaves you wide-eyed and open-mouthed. Caroline's story is one of these. As I read this book and learnt about the toxic abuse she endured, and as I look at her life now, I cannot help but worship Jesus. I cannot help but be wowed by His AMAZING grace at work in her life. She truly does live unrestrained!

I have the privilege of knowing Caroline personally. I see her pour out her love and devotion to Jesus in passionate worship. I hear her incredible stories of bold faith where she has prayed for people and seen them healed. I see her lead people and love people, and champion people to be all God has called them to be. Caroline is convinced of God's goodness and love, both for her and for others, and I find that so inspiring. It would have been so easy for Caroline's past to leave her broken and bitter. Instead, her life points to the kindness and unrivalled victory of Jesus. He is the saviour and the healer and the restorer, and Caroline's life shouts about these truths. She is a beacon of hope in a broken world and I know that her story will help many, many others to survive and thrive.

If you're currently trapped in an abusive relationship, let Caroline's story comfort you and bring you hope. If you've experienced abuse in the past and still live with the trauma of what you went through, let Caroline's story lead you into greater freedom. If you're supporting victims of abuse, let Caroline's story inspire faith in your heart that nothing is impossible with God. If you're someone who is fortunate enough to have never experienced abuse, let Caroline's story of redemption wow you and give you a deeper awe of God.

Whoever you are and whatever your circumstances, take your time over this book. Make the most of the opportunities to pause and reflect at the end of each chapter and allow the Holy Spirit to do what only He can. I know that God will honour Caroline's courage in writing this book. There is much freedom to come and hope to be imparted to all who read it. It is possible to survive and thrive after abuse.

It's time to live unrestrained!

Wendy Mann
Based at the King's Arms Church, Bedford, UK
Author of 'Naturally Supernatural' and 'Leading as Sons and Daughters'

Introduction

I sank back down into my seat having put my heart and soul into worship, eagerly anticipating all the speaker, Sophia Barrett, was about to say. I was at One Event on the Lincolnshire Showground and enjoying every moment of it. Working for Compassion UK had its perks and this was one of them. Once my project, the Compassion Experience, was closed for the day, I could pop into the meetings and, as I had at one time been part of the leadership team that organised this event, there was often a seat waiting for me. Having engaged with Father God, I was ready to receive all that Sophia had to say.

But our loving heavenly Father had other plans. Before she was even introduced, I felt the Holy Spirit speak to me quite clearly, "It's time to write a book about your experience of abuse." This was so unexpected. Out of the blue. Surely not? This was not something I had ever considered. I had put that part of my life behind me. As I reasoned with God, I became aware Sophia was being introduced and within a few minutes I realised what a gifted, talented, articulate and passionate speaker she was. How had I never heard her before? Even more surprising to me was that she referred to a book she had recently written called *Stay*. She went on to explain that this was about a dark period of her life when she had battled depression, anxiety, panic attacks and exhaustion. Not many leaders of large churches make themselves so vulnerable and yet this was powerful. Was God showing me what could be done? That sharing your journey of weakness could help others too?

Before I could even start thinking seriously about sharing my journey of surviving and thriving after abuse, I needed to gain the permission of my adult children – I would be describing their father in ways that they would surely find upsetting. I also wanted my mother's blessing, as I'd need to talk about my childhood too. I felt sure I wouldn't get past these obstacles but to my surprise, all agreed I could go ahead, even though the children said they probably wouldn't read it which was totally understandable. In addition, their father was no longer alive, so I was free to write without fear of retribution.

Within a few weeks of starting, I stopped. Memories, along with all their associated emotions, resurfaced and I just found it far too difficult. I couldn't do it, even though I had a sense that sharing my journey would be a comfort to those who shared similar experiences.

At that time, I embarked on a course called Training for Supernatural Ministry (tsmbedford.org). It was wonderful and I grew in courage and gifting, reaching out to people I came across in my everyday life, hearing from God for them, showing them the immense love and care of the Father through words of knowledge and prophetic encouragement. It was such an exciting time of my life. During this almost year long course, my understanding of who I was as the Father's daughter expanded and deepened. I experienced new levels of freedom and intimacy with God. I now serve on the leadership team for the course and continue to grow personally and help others press into all Father God has for them. As I came to the end of my TSM year, I felt prompted to have another go at writing this book. I found that as I was falling asleep some nights, I would remember an abusive incident from my past and see how I could write about it and then feel able to do so the next morning. I made some progress. The whole process of writing became easier and eventually even enjoyable.

I love my large family. I have five children and some of them have children of their own too! It's wonderful! Working full time while offering my family support in all sorts of ways, as well as moving house from one city to another and being involved in church, doesn't really leave much time for writing though. Having written almost nothing for a number of months, I found myself having an internal conversation with God about this book. "I'm not even really sure you told me to write it. I think I made it up. I've had a number of prophetic words over the last two years and not one of them has said anything about writing a book. I can't fit it into my life – I just don't have enough time! So I'm going to stop and not write another thing unless you tell me otherwise really clearly!"

Three days later, while I was clearing away the last of the cake at our annual TSM Graduation event, a tall man walked over to me and said, "Have you written that book yet?" I had not met him before and assumed he must have come with one of the graduates. He hadn't introduced himself and I didn't know his name. The first words to come out of my mouth were, "Why are you asking me that?" He ignored my question and went on to tell me I should make sure there is a head and shoulders photo of me in the book and then walked out of the glass doors onto the car park. How bizarre, I thought! Father God definitely had my attention now! I knew I had better get writing. Three weeks later, by the way, I bumped into the man in church – we usually went to different services. He didn't let me off the hook – I was asked how much I had written and given suggestions for carving out more time! God is gracious and kind and meets us even in our unbelief!

As I wrote the last few chapters of this book, I was assailed with thoughts of unworthiness. Our enemy would want me to believe that what I was writing is of no significance and will not be of any good to anyone: that it is waffle and has no substance. I have come to realise it's always a battle when you're stepping out in obedience and making yourself vulnerable.

I am believing as I share from my life you will see that it is possible not only to be a survivor of abuse but that you can actually thrive! Jesus came so that you and I can live abundant lives, full to overflowing with peace and joy (John 10:10). Where we once experienced control, oppression, containment and restraint, we can now live powerful, expansive and nurtured lives full of freedom and grace. We once felt bereft of hope and destined to live our lives on mute, but our God will reignite the flames of hope and give us a place and space to thrive. The mute button will not only be released, the sound will be on full volume. We will have a voice! We can and will live unrestrained lives!

CHAPTER ONE

Unrestrained – Cast off Shame

I just need to keep praying and walking. Please don't come back. Please Lord, keep him away. Don't let him come back. Ever. Even if that means death. In an accident perhaps or a heart attack. Don't let him come back. Yes, let him die. Quickly, quietly. A fatal accident. That will do it. I want this all to be over. I want to feel again, be rid of this numbness, this heaviness, this load. Rid of being on high alert, anticipating the worst, second guessing what's going to happen next.

This morning was another awful morning. I could do nothing right, as usual, but there was more this time. He had a plan and he was determined to convince me of it. A plan that involved having another woman introduced into our relationship, our marriage relationship. Did he really think I would agree? Did he think he had worn me down sufficiently, that I would quietly concede defeat? We argued, back and forth. No, it was not alright. It would never happen while I was in the house. It didn't matter that Solomon had 700 wives and loads of concubines. This was not Old Testament times. And then came the retribution. My punishment for not giving in. Car keys were taken so I couldn't go to work. My boss was called and told I would not be coming back to work – ever. The phone was locked so I couldn't call anyone. My books were taken away. My make-up hidden. I was to have this day with no distractions – time to reconsider. We'd talk when he came home.

So I kept walking around the swimming pool, praying. It was warm and the sun shone brightly. A beautiful day, really. I didn't honestly expect God to answer my ungodly prayers. Yet, I half hoped he would. I would be freer, lighter. I would have a life again! My mind was in turmoil, replaying every sentence spoken. He couldn't really think this ridiculous idea would come to anything, could he? Who was he thinking of bringing into *my* home with *my* children? He must be having an affair. Why else would he be raising ideas like this? The children! Just the thought of them, and the harm this would do, sent shots of adrenaline through my body. I would not allow it! Come hell or high water!

I realised I should eat something but couldn't. There was too much to think about, to consider. He would, inevitably, be home soon and I would need to manage him. Food for him, that would help. I'd start the coffee as I heard him arrive. A plate of meat, rice, two veg ready within minutes. There would be ructions if he were hungry and had to wait even half an hour. I'd pretend nothing had happened, that there was nothing to discuss. I'd be pleasant, helpful, smile a lot, kind, considerate. Hopefully, this would settle him.

Early evening came around all too soon. I had spent the day reading my Bible, the only book left to me, and praying. God was good and kind. A loving heavenly Father who was looking out for me. I reminded myself to take courage, to encourage myself in the Lord. He was my strength, my shield, my fortress, a very present help in times of trouble. I ran to him, lay at his feet on my bedroom floor and prayed, soaking in his comfort and his presence.

He arrived home with the children, all four of them, having collected the boys from school and the girls from pre-school.

There was the usual clamour and chaos of sorting out where four sets of books, bags, PE kit and lunch tins would settle: "Not there, in your bedroom, please!" Excitedly, the events of the day were recounted, each child vying for airtime, as usual. "I can only hear one of you at a time! Come and talk to me while I make dinner." I punctuated the chatter with the occasional affirmation or question and avoided answering honestly the awkward question as to why Daddy had picked them up. "I just had so much to do today," was an easy cop-out and no comparison with what I would say to explain the presence of another woman permanently in our home. Pushing that thought away, I set the table and dished up dinner. I was dreading the children going to bed – all would be well until then, superficially at least.

As I suspected, he wanted to continue the discussion he had started earlier once we were in our bedroom, where we couldn't be heard. He sat down in one of the bedroom armchairs, leant back with linked fingers across his chest, legs bent at the knees and feet apart. Fixing his eyes on my face, the inquisition started, calmly, measured: Had I taken time to reconsider? What were my objections? What scriptural basis did I have for my arguments? The marriage bed is undefiled! Emotions started running higher, voices became louder. He stood up and walked over to where I was standing, right in front of me. He pointed a finger in my face, touching my nose, jabbing it. Sneering. Despite determined effort, my voice broke, exasperation apparent and tears rolled down my face. I moved away, angry, shouting out my resistance. He grabbed my arm and violently threw me onto the bed. "You will do as I say! I am your lord. You will call me lord as Sarah called Abraham lord."

I had asked him, pleaded with him not to have sex while angry, but with no effect. Eventually, I just lay there, accepting it. I pretended it wasn't me that this was happening to. I was on the outside, looking in, observing. Letting him just get on until it was all over. Until he was spent. Anger dissipated. Calm. Then the remorse would come – and it did. "I'm sorry. You know I love you. There is no-one else for me. Let me hold you, be close to you. This will never happen again. Forgive me."

I was up first, knowing I needed to get the children to school. As I opened the bedroom door, I noticed a small piece of white paper trapped under it. I removed it carefully, making sure I didn't tear it. It read, "Daddy shouts, Mummy cries." My heart sank.

―――――――――――◆◇◆―――――――――――

"Shame is a soul eating emotion."[1]

Carl Gustav Jung

I went into this marriage with a sense of shame. I had been a Christian since I was nearly six years old and had sought to love and obey God through my teen years too. I finished school having just turned seventeen and started training to be a nurse. The first thing I did when I moved into the nurses' residence, nearly an hour's drive away from home, was to find a church. My heart was set on being part of a Christian community and serving God.

Three months into my training, I met him and we were married nine months later. I didn't say my wedding vows as

―――――――――――――――――――――――――――――――――――――――

1. The Red Book: A Reader's Edition (Philemon), Carl Gustav Jung, 2012, W.W. Norton & Co.

a virgin as I had hoped. Yes, he had seduced me but equally I blamed myself too as I was curious about sex. I cried for three full days after that first sexual act and then decided that this meant I would have to marry him. After all, how would I ever explain what had happened to someone else if I didn't marry him? Having made that decision, I missed the signs that all was not well, that perhaps someone less naïve and less adamant may have noticed. He had a mean streak but I chose to ignore it. He insisted, after that first time, on having sex whenever and wherever it suited him even if I was menstruating. When we were in public or with his family, he would continuously have his arm around me, pulling me close to him, often kissing me in an intimate way in front of others. People noticed and commented but that just fuelled his obsessive behaviour towards me. If I pulled away, he would pull me closer. We argued all the time but he always won. In the weeks before our wedding, I spoke to him about delaying it as we had had another argument, but he convinced me this would be inconveniencing so many people and that wouldn't be fair. So we went ahead.

The abuse started on honeymoon. We were having sex at least three times a day, even when I didn't want to. My protestations were met with firm arm grips and emotional slurs. The whole two weeks were almost exclusively about his sexual satisfaction. My sense of shame deepened. I felt like I was being used. I blamed myself. If I hadn't had sex before we got married, I wouldn't have been in this situation. I couldn't immediately work out how to make things right. So I tried hard to please him, to gain his approval.

I didn't realise that shame was becoming part of who I was. Over the years, the sense of shame intensified. I felt ashamed of the fact that I allowed him to use me as he did, even though rationally I knew I was trying to preserve my family. After one occasion when he persuaded me through intimidation to have anal sex, shame so pervaded my mind the next day that I seriously considered suicide. On another occasion while on holiday, I felt humiliated and shamed as he read pornographic magazines on a public train while I was with him. In addition to these specific instances, there was the daily grind of hearing that I was not good enough as a mother, as a home maker, as a wife. That I needed to learn other ways of being, as being myself was insufficient. Alongside the sexual misuse and abuse, this meant that shame became part of my very being – part of my every tissue.

I compartmentalised my life so that this deep sense of shame wasn't apparent in my work and church life. There I worked at being confident, effective and accomplished. When he wasn't around, I could be a different person and block out any other thoughts and feelings. This often worked, although not always. It took a lot of energy to maintain this, although it didn't always feel like an act as I was inherently a confident and capable person. It was keeping all other thoughts at bay that was more difficult and took so much effort.

It wasn't until years after I had left this marriage that I came face to face with the shame I felt. For me, self blame and shame went hand in hand. I had to forgive myself for all the things I blamed myself for. I had to recognise and accept that pre-marital sex was not an unforgivable sin that resulted in punishment. The blood of Jesus and the grace and mercy of God are so much more powerful than any sin I have ever committed. I am a child of Father God and cleansed from all (yes all!) unrighteousness. I had not caused the abuse I had endured. I had no part in making it happen. Wow! That was liberating. And it became a reality to me as I walked to the front of a church during a Cleansing Stream session (cleansingstream.org) to symbolically wash shame from my face.

No child of God needs to carry shame and self-blame. There is no condemnation to those who love God (Romans 8:1). These are enemy tactics to keep us from experiencing true freedom. Jesus carried every single ounce of shame on himself for us on the cross. Shame doesn't need to be carried or paid for twice! We can all be free from shame. Jesus lifts our heads so we can look him, others and the world in the eyes. He loves us so very much that he endured a torturous death for us so we don't have to torture ourselves. We are his pride and joy! He loves the way we love him and delight in all he is leading us into. It's good to let go of shame and embrace freedom!

Pause and Reflect

We have all made mistakes and harmful choices. These don't need to define who you are though. You can recover. You can be restored. You can experience the love and care of a heavenly Father, his enduring forgiveness and have all the mirk and muck washed away.

1. Are there mistakes and bad choices you've made that you blame yourself for? Take a moment and ask the Holy Spirit to show you what these may be.

2. Write each of these down on a piece of paper and spread them out in prayer before Father God.

3. Thank him for the sacrifice of Jesus Christ, his son, that has already paid the price for all these mistakes, all these wrong choices.

4. Know that our Father is drawing close to you – he loves it when you come to him just as you are. Receive his love and forgiveness. Allow it to soak into your very being.

Forgive yourself – if the God of the universe forgives you, you are worthy of your own forgiveness too.

5. Gather together all the pieces of paper and prayerfully tear them into tiny pieces and throw them away (or burn them).

6. In Psalm 103: 6-12 (Message Translation) we are told:

> God makes everything come out right;
> he puts victims back on their feet.
> He showed Moses how he went about his work,
> opened up his plans to all Israel.
> God is sheer mercy and grace;
> not easily angered, he's rich in love.
> He doesn't endlessly nag and scold,
> nor hold grudges forever.
> He doesn't treat us as our sins deserve,
> nor pay us back in full for our wrongs.
> As high as heaven is over the earth,
> so strong is his love to those who fear him.
> And as far as sunrise is from sunset,
> he has separated us from our sins.

Remind yourself of how loved you are every day for the next month. Read this as often as you can and smile when you remember that Father God is sheer mercy and grace and that he has separated you from all the things you blamed yourself for – as far as the east is from the west!

CHAPTER TWO

Unrestrained – Experience Anger

He sat on the dark leather sofa with a large glass of brandy in his hand. It was obvious he was enjoying it. He swirled it in its glass, held his nose over it and sniffed, took small sips, and then leant back in his seat, letting out an almost inaudible breath of air. The children were seated behind him at an elevated breakfast bar, fussing and chattering. The boys finished their lunch, clambered down and ran off to play outside. The girls, being only five years old, took so much longer to eat while they played about in between mouthfuls. Inevitably, I suppose, a cup of orange juice was knocked over and spilled. Before I could get to it, the juice had spread across the narrow breakfast bar and was running over the edge and onto their father's head!

Any semblance of family harmony was immediately destroyed. Loud expletives echoed across the room. The boys came running to the door. Within seconds he had the culprit by the shoulders, having yanked her off her stool. His face was only an inch from hers: red and angry. "What do you think you are f***ing doing? Stupid! Careless! F***ing stupid!" Her initial shocked silence gave way to hysterical crying at this point. Frenetically, I pushed my face in between his and hers while putting all my weight on his arms, trying to move them off her. This worked partially. In reality, my actions served only as a distraction. In a blur, I used one hand to put her onto the floor on her feet while I was being forcibly dragged away by my other hand. I then pushed back, resisted, fell down. Momentarily he let go and then immediately grabbed my hair, dragging me down the passage way, all the while telling me I had to be taught a lesson. Struggling, I pleaded and cried. The children followed, crying too. Within a few moments we were outside and I realised I was being flung into the swimming pool. Humiliated and distraught, I felt my feet on the bottom of the pool and pushed myself up to the surface.

Remarkably composed, he had summoned the children to himself, his back to me and the pool. I could hear him explaining that this was a game. That Mummy wasn't hurt. That she just needed to cool down and calm down. He took them inside with the promise of ice cream.

I gathered my thoughts as I stripped off, dried and changed. This was new. This was different. He hadn't sworn and screamed in the face of the girls before. He usually kept any physical violence towards me for when the children weren't around. He had also only recently begun drinking brandy at home on a regular basis and only sometimes during the day. He was never pleasant after brandy. He was always more aggressive, far more confrontational. It seemed to unleash anything that was lurking beneath the surface. I always tried to stay out of his way, or mitigate whatever I could, when he was drinking brandy. But I hadn't seen this coming today. I hadn't realised the children could be involved, impacted, traumatised.

Picking up my car keys, I calmly and purposefully walked towards the front door, past him and the children as they sat on the sofas eating ice cream and watching a movie. "I'm going to the shops for treats. I'll be back soon." No-one moved. They were absorbed.

I stopped in the parking lot of our church, in one of the periphery spaces away from prying eyes or concerned glances.

I needed a few quiet moments with my Father God – just me and him. I was raw and hurting. Yes, my body ached: my muscles were taut and tight with stress. But my soul was feeling the effects too. Days, weeks, months, years of uncertainty and anticipation of the worst was leaving its mark. My soul felt ripped, torn, shredded in places. I was doing all I could to protect myself by being alert to his moods and whims but it wasn't working very well. I felt like giving up but I didn't even know what that would look like. If only I could breathe my last breath and go to be with the Father – just float away. But my children, my beautiful children. What would become of them?

Weeping, I felt the comfort and care of the Father envelop me. I was loved, had always been loved – since my mother's womb. Jesus had always been with me. I didn't walk this path alone. Strength and peace, resilience and composure seemed to seep into every cell of my body, soul and spirit. I sat still without moving for some time, welcoming the healing that was taking place. Eventually, I began to pray. Out loud. For myself. For my children. For him. I felt indignation and passion, perseverance and courage rise up on the inside of me. I was a daughter of the King of kings! I could walk through water and through fires with him by my side. I would not be moved! My life was built on the solid rock of Jesus Christ! I was his and he was mine! I would not succumb to threats! I would not be intimidated! I would not be moved! I was immovable!

Having gained perspective once more, I realised that almost an hour had passed and I still needed to shop for treats. I planned ahead – I would walk back into the house, bags in my hand and head straight for the kitchen to unpack the things I had bought. It would be as if nothing had happened.

"Anger ventilated often hurries towards forgiveness; and concealed often hardens into revenge."[2]

Edward G. Bulwer-Lytton

Anger can make itself known in an individual's life in so many different ways. For me, the first four years of my marriage, I fought and struggled to make myself heard. I tried saying no to having sex when I didn't want it but this ended in threats, intimidation and physical restraint. The end result was always that he got what he wanted anyway. I did rail against this but to no avail. Sometimes I was pushed out of the front door of the flat we were living in, dressed in night clothes only, and locked out until I saw sense. After hours of crying, knocking and asking to be let in, I would walk away and find a spot to shelter in and cry until daylight. I didn't cause a scene as I was ashamed of what was happening and didn't want the neighbours to know. Looking back, I think they must have heard something but they never intervened in any way. Once it was daylight, he would let me back into the flat as I don't think he wanted anyone to see me outside either.

This response to the manipulation and abuse was exhausting – emotionally and physically – and it had no effect whatsoever on him. He prided himself on winning arguments and wasn't happy for me to have opinions different from his at all. So even in everyday matters, he would twist and turn what I was saying until I agreed with him. He boasted that he could make anyone believe the sun was shining even in the middle of the

---

2. (25 May 1803 -18 January 1873). He coined the phrases "the great unwashed", "pursuit of the almighty dollar", "the pen is mightier than the sword", and "dweller on the threshold". The Life Letters and Literary Remains of Edward Bulwer, Lord Lytton V1, Edward Bulwer Lytton, 2010, Kessinger Publishing.

night. I remember a male friend at church asking how married life was treating me and, when I hesitated, quickly saying that the first years were always the worst and things would get better. Another friend once told me her married sister said that marriage was worth it as long as the happy times outnumbered the struggles. I reminded myself often that the first few years were bound to be tough as we adapted to one another and braced myself for the next argument or worse. When things got bad, I would count the days I was happy and the days that were bad and as long as there were more happy than bad days, I felt consoled.

He was also very jealous and possessive. Once at a family wedding, his older brother asked me to dance while he was out of the room. At first I refused, saying I couldn't dance, but he insisted. When my husband returned to see me dancing with his brother, he was furious. As I went to sit down, he grabbed my arm and marched me to the door. We were leaving. I defended myself as robustly as I dared – we were in full view of all the guests. I explained that I couldn't have refused to dance without being impolite or causing a scene. But my words fell on deaf ears. That turned out to be a bad night.

I found the ongoing raised voice arguments, the physical, sexual and emotional abuse followed by hours of crying, absolutely exhausting. I started having nightmares where I was naked, bruised and bleeding standing alone in the wind and rain with an empty and torn purse. Almost at the end of myself, I decided to stop railing, arguing, crying. I would give in, do whatever he wanted from me, be a good wife and mother. For the most part, I managed to bury the tears or keep them for when I was alone. I didn't realise that I had also locked away the anger that continued to build up.

A few years into my marriage to my kind and compassionate second husband, I found myself boiling over with anger towards him over small things. We had a wise, older lady in church who was a counsellor in her day job. She and I had a long chat and she immediately pointed out that I wasn't angry with my new husband but rather that the anger I was directing at him had its source elsewhere. I had denied that anger for so many years, supressing it to a place where I no longer knew that it existed. But any emotional response that is denied and contained eventually has to surface and be dealt with. Not only was I angry with my abusive husband for the abuse and misuse he had put me through, I was angry with God for letting it happen. That came as a shock to me. I was, after all, getting on with my life – in a good relationship, healed up and doing well.

While participating in a few counselling sessions, I came before God and made my anger toward both the abusive husband and God himself known. I didn't hold back. David in the Bible had shouted at God many times and yet God loved him so much he called him "a man after God's own heart". Father God could cope with my questions and accusations. I allowed all the anger I felt to surface and spill out. Some of the language I used was not savoury! Once again, I forgave the abusive husband and then I forgave God too. I recognise that there is mystery in this walk we walk with our loving heavenly Father. I can't say I understand everything and why it happened. I do know some good came out of it – four children, my own spiritual growth and more. I gave up my right to know and understand why on this side of heaven though. Father God is faithful.

Pause and Reflect

It really is OK to be angry about the things that have happened to you. In a perfect world, none of it would have happened. And no-one has the right to abuse and misuse another human being. You are worth so much more. Many of us don't like to get angry – we feel it's not culturally or socially acceptable. Anger that's not released (in a safe space) can eat away at you from the inside out and may even make you physically ill. You may feel unable to express anger or even be concerned that doing so might be wrong and could hurt you or someone else. The following tips may help you give expression to anger in a safe way:

1. Take a moment to think about something hurtful that you have experienced. Now imagine that being done to someone else. If, by chance, you saw that situation happening right before your own eyes, how would you feel? I suspect that anger would rise up within you. You would want to prevent it from continuing. You may want to take strong physical action to rescue that person. You may even be shouting or screaming as you did so. Think about that. You have the right to feel just as angry about that happening to you. It should never have happened. It wasn't right.

2. I have found that the more I process my anger about the abuse and the injustice of it with Father God, the less I find myself lashing out at odd times about comparatively insignificant things. Nothing I say to God shocks or surprises him. He can handle it all and more! He doesn't even mind if I blame him for things that he didn't cause, do or didn't do. Many of the Psalms are full of questions and harsh, raw emotions such as anger – and those thoughts, feelings and prayers made it into the Bible!

3. Find a safe place (a room or space where you won't be bothered or distracted) and get alone with Father God (or include a prayer partner).

4. Pour out your heart. Let yourself experience the anger you've bottled up for so long. Get it out!

5. Once you feel you have fully vented anger in that moment (you may want to do this again at a different time, remembering a different situation), call to remembrance just how loved you are, what a blessing God has created you to be, how much you delight the Father and that you are worth so much more than many treasures. Allow yourself to bask in the knowledge of how much you are loved by our Father God.

6. Lastly, put your eyes back on the face of Jesus and thank him for all he is doing in and through you.

CHAPTER THREE

Unrestrained – Step into Authenticity

Today looked like it was going to be a good day. Yesterday had not been a good day. When I was first married, I'd count the good and bad days and, as long as there were more good than bad ones, I thought I was doing OK. It wasn't always that easy to distinguish between a good and a bad day though. It could start out OK and become disastrous – for me at least. I had grown in my ability to discern his frame of mind and moods. I had learnt to manage the environment to promote a good mood day. If I was unsuccessful, if something I said or did displeased him, if someone else unsettled him, then I could be in for a troubled night.

Sometimes it was a small thing that annoyed him. I had made his coffee cup too full or it was not full enough. It could be too hot or not hot enough. His dissatisfaction always reflected back onto me – it was my fault. I was deliberately trying to make him spill that coffee, or deprive him of a good long drink, or make him burn his lips, or spoil his enjoyment by giving him cold coffee. I was at fault. Not up to even making a decent cup of coffee. The day may have started well and then this one small thing would turn it all on its head. Within minutes, he could be teasing and raucously laughing with the children. In his more reflective moments, he would boast about being "like the wind", switching from one mood to another within minutes many times within a day.

This was normal, day to day life for me and I managed to make the most of it – most of the time. I compartmentalised my life so I could enjoy as fully as possible the other parts of it. I loved my children, my church life, my work and my relationship with God. I was often promoted to leadership positions in church and work. I studied hard and gained a few degrees. These other successes helped me to maintain a sense of who I was during the bad days and also the better days when I was able to manage things there too.

The really good times at home always came after a really bad time, in fact they usually started the very next day. Probably sensing that he had gone too far, he would treat me well. Run my bath, make me a cup of tea, put the children to bed, tell me he loved me, bring me flowers. I accepted all of this graciously, knowing it would be short lived. If I didn't expect too much, I wouldn't be disappointed. If this spat of good days followed the usual pattern, it would last for two to three weeks at the very most and then things would change. Faults would be found, holes picked, nasty words spoken, insults hurled until it disintegrated into degenerative viciousness. Usually about a week long of maliciousness. These weeks broke me. They tore at my soul and left me gasping for breath. And as the space between them became shorter and shorter, I was finding it increasingly difficult to recover sufficiently to cope with the next bout.

But this seemed to be a good day. I had prayed fervently yesterday and again this morning. I couldn't fast today as it was the weekend and I would have to explain and I couldn't. But I had prayed for him this morning and was praying for him in between the normal everyday tasks. I'd known for some time that prayer could affect his mood swings. There was a spiritual dimension to them. When in a place of prayer, I felt compassion well up for him and prayers came from my heart. He seemed more at peace today, more content.

After lunch, he went to sit outside with a glass of brandy. Recently, he had taken to keeping a bottle or two at home, close to hand. I was teetotal. My heart sank as he sipped away. It was still so early and, as I suspected, one drink led to another. However, he was still mellow and congenial so there was hope for a peaceful evening. At about four o'clock he unexpectedly stood up, announced he was going out and left without answering any of the questions I was asking.

This did not bode well. As early evening came, I settled the children into baths, television and then beds, not wanting them up and about when he arrived home. I needn't have worried as he didn't come in until the early hours of the morning, albeit very drunk and aggressive. I pretended to be sleeping but he shook me until I woke up. He didn't want coffee or a bath. It seemed he just wanted to make sure I understood he did all these things because I drove him to it. His drunkenness was my doing – I had caused it. Eventually I agreed with him. It was all my fault. He agreed to lie down and sleep and talk in the morning. I was very relieved. We both slept.

"Authenticity is more than speaking; authenticity is also about doing. Every decision we make says something about who we are."[3]

Simon Sinek

It's taken me a while to understand why I didn't take anyone into my confidence during all those years of abuse. Even now, I'm still gaining insight as part of my journey with Father God.

In my formative years, I had lived with a parent who was themselves just beyond childhood and away from supportive, wise input from older family members. It can't have been easy raising a family of four young children in a foreign country where customs were different. My mother was changeable and easily angered when she was younger. Being married to a man who could go through four or five moods within a day was similar but far more intense. My learned coping strategies just fell into place once more. This became my "normal" again. If I did get upset and argue that things shouldn't be this way, that I should be treated properly and that I had a right to want things to be done differently, I was told that the way he did things was the normal way and it was me who was being difficult. I was only just eighteen when we married and hadn't seen a variety of marriages up close, except my own parents, and theirs had been volatile at times. So eventually I accepted that he was right – this was normal.

As a young woman, I went into this marriage with a somewhat romantic idea of what life would be like. The fact that I was finding it to be far from this made me feel like a failure. I was obviously not doing what needed to be done to be properly loved and nurtured. A deep sense of failure and

---

3.   Start with Why: How Great Leaders Inspire Everyone to Take Action, Simon Sinek, 2011, Penguin.

self blame meant I didn't feel like I wanted to tell anyone what was happening at home. Other people knowing would just deepen my sense of shame at my own inadequacies. Effectively, I deliberately hid this part of my life from others.

I wanted to be seen as competent and effective. I was hardworking and conscientious so this wasn't too difficult. I have been blessed with an ability to focus on a task at hand to the exclusion of other things. I am not easily distracted – unless I want to be. This, together with being a ready learner, has led to success in most things that I put my mind to. It also helped me to segregate my life into different sections, each with its own personalised criteria for success. I wasn't making a success of my marriage, I told myself, but I was making a success of work and church jobs. I may not be competent at home but I was in other areas of my life. To others I appeared confident, outgoing, optimistic, successful, organised, effective. I didn't want anyone to know what was happening at home because then I may have been viewed as a victim – someone who was helpless with no control over their lives. This was indeed what I felt like on the inside when I gave myself permission to slow down and reflect, but it was not what I wanted others to think of me.

As a child I had learned to keep myself busy. Being busy meant I was accomplishing something and this made me feel good about myself. Often, it also pleased someone else when I got something done for them. On top of that, it kept my mind and thoughts occupied. While I was working and busy, I only thought of what I was doing. There was no space for contemplating the relationships I was in or the state of my life. This strategy served me well while I was in an abusive marriage. I became known as someone who could get things done at work and church. I was good at gathering people and motivating them around a task or project. Talking about what was happening at home would have destroyed the view others had of me – or so I believed. So I kept it all to myself.

I did cry out to God and ask him to change my circumstances. To me, it was just God and me – no-one else needed to know. I spent seasons of fasting and praying. I stood in faith and proclaimed freedom over him and our marriage. I wrote out scriptures and read them many times each day. It felt to me like the days I prayed vehemently would be good days, his moods would be more stable. But if I skipped a day, he would erupt and a cycle of abuse would begin again.

A number of times I came to a point when I thought I couldn't go on. I'd ask him to come with me to see a counsellor and sometimes he would agree. I'd make an appointment, as then he would treat me well in the days and sometimes weeks before we went to it. However, with a day or two to go, he'd convince me that we didn't need to go after all. Look at how well we were doing. We didn't need any help. All would be well now. I may as well cancel the appointment as he wouldn't go anyway – we had a good marriage.

Looking back, I realise it could only have done me good had I chosen to speak to someone (or maybe more than one person) much earlier on. I didn't seem to be able to. It took the insightful intervention of the Dean of the Bible School we were attending to help me share what was happening for the very first time. I'm grateful to God for the grace and care he extended towards me at that point and for the wisdom in insisting that I needed the intervention of a counsellor which he then arranged for me. I'm also grateful that meeting with him became the beginning of a journey of living as authentically as I am able to day by day. It was the beginning of removing the mask I wore daily, of allowing myself to be visibly broken.

Pause and Reflect

It can be a really scary thing to take off our masks and let others see us for who we really are. This usually doesn't happen in one single, gigantic step. There are so many reasons for hiding the pain you are going through. I didn't want to be seen as a victim or have people look at me in pity. There was also the fear of physical, mental and emotional retribution if he found out that I was telling anyone else about what was going on. Fear is a powerful motivation for self-preservation. I felt that if I kept praying and stayed silent, pretending that all was as it should be, it would get better and no-one need ever know. In addition, when others only see the charming, friendly side of the abuser, there is the fear of not being believed, others thinking you are exaggerating or not emotionally balanced. Authenticity feels like a no-win situation.

Without authenticity, however, there is no freedom. We have to learn to be who we truly are. Being authentic and vulnerable step by step, one decision at a time, is easier when we do so from a place of knowing we are completely accepted and loved by Father God. There is no one quite like you. You are distinctively and uniquely you and that is so good! Father God absolutely delights in you – after all, he gave you all your gifts and talents because he likes them. Here is an exercise to help you in your journey of learning to be authentic and vulnerable with yourself, others and Father God.

1. Take a moment to describe what you look like. Tall or short? Long hair or short? Straight or curly? Colour of eyes, hair, skin? Glasses, contacts or not? What else? Anything unusual?

2. Make a list of the things you like doing. Cooking, cleaning, running, drawing, writing, eating, dancing, music, reading and so on.

3. What about your personality? Reflective, quiet, outgoing, talkative?

4. What are your strengths? Make people feel at ease? Good at organising things? Passionate about children, making cakes, building things?

   If you can't come up with a list in response to any or all of the points above, ask someone who knows you well and enjoys being with you to tell you how they see you in response to the points above. Jot down all the ideas onto a piece of paper and then find a mirror.

5. Look at yourself in the mirror and read out loud to yourself the complete description of yourself as you have it written down. Add the sentence at the end, "I am so glad Father God made me this way." It may well feel a bit awkward at first but practise a few times until you can do it. For example, I could say, "I am a short woman with silver curly hair and blue eyes. I wear glasses and have a roundish face with only a few lines on it! I love gardening, enjoy reading and writing. I am outgoing and talkative with a bubbly personality. I am positive and love children. I am great at organising things and helping people grow and develop. I am so glad Father God has made me this way."

6. Once you've done that, take another step on this journey of authenticity. Look in the mirror, read the following statements out loud to yourself (keep trying until you can look yourself in the eye while saying these things):

   I am a child of God (John 1:12)

   I am holy and blameless (Ephesians 1:4)

   I am chosen and dearly loved by Father God (Colossians 3:12)

   God sings songs of rejoicing over me. He delights in me, just as I am. (Zephaniah 3:17)

CHAPTER FOUR

Unrestrained – Forgive the Inexcusable

I hadn't been in this first floor office before and it was impressive. To my left was a large dark wood boardroom table, big enough to seat at least twelve people. The windows to my right looked out over green lawns and flower beds – all carefully manicured. A peaceful setting. We sat down next to each other but on separate chairs, looking across a large desk at the pastoral counsellor. He was second in charge of this large, 16,000-member church. And we were part of the 500 strong Bible Training Centre housed on site.

The counsellor wasted no time. Looking straight at me, he asked me to give my version of events. And so I did. It wasn't easy: I felt disloyal. However, it was now or never, wasn't it? It had been difficult to get him to come here with me. I had tried to persuade him that marriage counselling would be good for us so many times before but, after agreeing, he had flatly refused. On a few occasions he had agreed and then pulled out a day or so before the appointment. So, right up to the last moment, I had thought he may not turn up. While he was here I needed to say all that I could, knowing he wouldn't be allowed to silence me. I spoke about the physical intimidation and threatening behaviour, the emotional coercion and manipulation, the sexual demands and perversion, the psychological batterings. I gave examples. It took a while. At times I needed to pause and collect myself before carrying on. I was acutely aware of him sitting only a few inches from me – was he about to explode any moment now? He didn't. In fact, he barely moved. He seemed relaxed and at ease. Almost nonchalant. "Is there anything you would like to correct?" he was asked as I came to a halt. "No, nothing. She is mine. Her body is mine. I can do what I like with her. It's my right."

Motionless and silent, my eyes firmly fixed on the counsellor, I waited for him to respond. Although his face was expressionless, I sensed he was gathering his thoughts and preparing a response to this unexpected statement. Remembering he was Mediterranean by birth, I wondered if he was suppressing a desire to shout or jump up. After what was probably only a few seconds (but felt like many minutes), he spoke out a number of questions in quick succession, pausing very briefly between each for an answer that didn't materialise: Would Jesus treat your wife as you have? Do your actions demonstrate you laying down your life for her? Is that the way you would treat your own body? Which aspects of Godly love are you showing her? The counsellor leant forward, elbows on the desk and waited.

He began his defence. Scripture was taken out of context, twisted and used to substantiate his arguments. My part in this session was over. All I could do was watch the exchange and wait for the outcome. It soon became apparent that the counsellor was more than able to unpick his reasoning – he was backing him into a corner. Would he own up? Would he admit things would need to change? Could he make that leap?

Both men were on their feet, heading for the door: one escaping, the other pleading. Suddenly, as the door was opened, the counsellor fell to his knees and flung his arms around the other's knees, begging him to stay, to talk. Shocked, I could barely take it all in. This was not traditional counselling practice! This desperate attempt to save our relationship seemed to throw him into temporary confusion, buying the counsellor a few more moments to convince him to stay, all the while holding onto his legs thus preventing him from moving through the half open door. And then it happened – he turned around. Quickly and quietly, the counsellor leant over, pushed the door closed, stood up and walked with him back to his chair, hand on his shoulder.

He was quieter, subdued. The counsellor thanked him for giving our relationship another chance. He suggested that he see us separately the next time. In a last defiant gesture, he agreed, only if I would spend some sessions with the counsellor's wife, who could show me what it was like to be a good wife. It was agreed. He also agreed to meet one-to-one with the counsellor the following day. Needing to get back to work, he made his way to the door, leaving me behind, still in my chair.

The counsellor came and sat in a chair close to me, took my hands in his and prayed for me: the peace, comfort, protection of Father God. There would be no meeting with his wife. Laughingly, he said she was fiery and would tell me to leave immediately. We would meet again the day after tomorrow.

Outside, I felt lighter somehow. I had been believed. This was not a normal way to live. Women were not treated like this in loving, honouring relationships. I had an ally. A person with authority, a person who elicited respect, a person who could present coherent and convincing arguments, a person who was passionate about marriage. Perhaps this would be a turning point. A new beginning for us.

◆◇◆

"To be a Christian means to forgive the inexcusable, because God has forgiven the inexcusable in you."[4]

C.S. Lewis

Forgiveness has to be the most difficult thing to do if you have been abused. I have heard many things said over the years about forgiveness and some have helped and others not. Forgiveness is a personal response and needs to be acted upon in a personal way, I feel.

Forgiving my mother for the way I was treated by her as a child wasn't too difficult for me because I understood the pressures she had been under. She was away from her family support network, my father was not supportive to her in her parenting, she had the pressure of living on little money, she was a very young mother with three, four, five then six children! She also wasn't a Christian while I was growing up – she became one when I was thirteen years old. At this stage she also gained the support of a church family and her life changed radically.

I remember sitting in a church service one Sunday when the speaker, at the end of the service, asked us all to close our eyes and ask God to show us if there was anyone we needed to forgive. I did so but fully expected there to be no-one. To my surprise, God showed me that I needed to forgive my mother. At this stage of my life I was a young mother with two children of my own and I was living an hour's drive away from where my mother lived. During the following week, I drove out to see her and we sat around her kitchen table and talked. I was apprehensive about talking about things from my childhood, but I needn't have been. My lovely mum listened and then

---

4. Mere Christianity, C.S. Lewis, 2012, William Collins.

shared her own recollections of events, accepted her own brokenness in those situations and then we prayed together. To this day we share our journeys with one another, praying for one another along the way.

Exercising forgiveness during many years in an abusive marriage played out differently. For me to survive emotionally and physically, I found I needed to forgive him continually and intentionally after each specific abusive incident. It was the only way I could let go of the emotional pain I physically experienced in my body. Each time it was an act of obedience. I would find time to come aside on my own while the children were at school or at a friend's place playing and he was not around for some reason. Sometimes it would be at work while I was on my own in my office. Lying on the floor, I would soften my heart before God and ask him to come as the Father of all Comfort and be with me. He always did. I would feel his presence all over me while I waited on him. And then I would ask God to help me forgive my then husband. I didn't feel I could go on as a wife and mother in the same house if I hadn't forgiven him so I needed God's help to do so. Looking back, I am aware that my motivations for forgiving were often selfish ones. I wanted to keep my children, I didn't feel like I could manage financially on my own, I didn't want to be a divorced woman and I was scared that he would kill me if I couldn't forgive him and therefore left. I know now that many of these reasons are common to so many abused people. They are some of the reasons we stay in abusive relationships. For me, I could only stay if I had forgiven him. He made it easier to forgive him during these years because he was always sorry after a specific abusive incident, often crying tears of remorse.

Once I had left him and I was on my own, I started realising just how abnormal my marriage had been. The abuse didn't stop, of course. He intimidated me almost daily, broke into my home and terrorised me over the course of a night, disobeyed a restraining order a few times by kicking my car, letting down my tyres and so forth. During this time, I was concentrating on getting myself healed from the inside. Father God is so full of kindness and grace that this healing takes place in stages, I found. We are not expected to go from brokenness to wholeness in one go. It happens layer upon layer. God shows us things that need to be dealt with a bit at a time. But somewhere in this process we do have to forgive as part of the healing and freedom process. And that's usually not easy!

Corrie ten Boom tells the story of coming face to face with a prison guard at the end of a meeting at which she was speaking. He had been a guard at the concentration camp where her sister had died a horrible death. He was one of the guards who had treated them very badly. Corrie could have been excused for scurrying off the platform and hiding behind the curtains. Instead of that, she was face to face with this abuser who was holding out his hand asking her for forgiveness. She says that the only thing she could do was obey Christ who asks us to forgive our enemies – she had no warm fuzzy feelings of forgiveness – so she reached out her hand and took his. What amazing courage! As Christians we are asked to obey because we love Jesus – no other reason. We are Christ followers and Jesus forgave those publicly who nailed him to a cross and watched him die.

In my case, I chose to obey and so I spoke forgiveness over him as well as blessing – we are told to bless those who curse us. This did not change him but it did change me. He continued to be mean and vindictive towards me over the years, as we had to have some contact because we had four children. Some years ago he died of cancer. In the weeks preceding his death, I called him to tell him that I wanted him to know that I had forgiven him for everything before he met God. His response was to say, "Forgive me? What for?"

Sometimes when we forgive, we are able to forge a stronger relationship with that person, as I did with my mother. Sometimes we forgive but we are never given the recognition or confirmation that a wrong was indeed perpetrated. This is more often the case where there has been an abusive relationship but we are still asked to forgive. And we do so because we love and trust Christ Jesus who showed us how.

Pause and Reflect

Forgiveness is not a feeling, it's a decision followed by an action. Practising forgiveness brings release and freedom to the one doing the forgiving even when it's not received (or even acknowledged) by the abuser. Forgiveness is not about freeing the abuser but about freeing yourself from the effects of resentfulness, bitterness and even hatred. Practising forgiveness does not mean you condone, excuse or accept the abusive behaviour. It also does not mean you have to be reconciled to the abuser. It's a choice to free yourself from the negative emotional ties with the abusive situation and person.

Once you have made the decision to forgive the person who abused or misused you, or even someone you think knew about the situation but didn't help or protect you, use the following exercise to help you to release them and set yourself free:

1. Before you start, ask Jesus to come into the room and be with you.

2. Then take a moment to picture a specific situation, and the person involved, when you were abused or misused.

3. Allow yourself to experience the emotions associated with that situation and person.

4. Express the emotions verbally if you like. Don't hold back.

5. Now see yourself putting the person into a boat and, while holding onto a rope attached to the boat, push the boat with the person in it out onto the water.

6. As the boat moves into the distance let go of the rope. Watch as it moves further and further away over the horizon and out of site.

7. While watching the boat move away, thank Jesus for being with you and helping you to do this. Make a decision to forgive the person in the boat and express that forgiveness out loud. Give them into the hands of Father God as you lose sight of them over the horizon.

Don't worry if you can't do this exercise completely the first time. A lovely friend of mine told me the first time she did this, all she could think of was setting the boat on fire! Jesus understands that! If that is you, then come back to this exercise and ask Father God to pour into you the ability to let this person go into the hands of Father God. This decision and act of letting go, of forgiving them (even if not accompanied by any emotions of forgiveness), will release you from the ties you have with them and the abusive situation. You will be free of it! Forgiveness is for your benefit!

CHAPTER FIVE

Unrestrained – Embrace Healing

I had enjoyed designing and furnishing the main bedroom. When we moved into this house, it was a double garage. Now it was a spacious bedroom with a dressing area, its own bathroom and glass patio doors leading out on to the garden. One wall was papered in impressionistic, soft pink and grey flowers. Together with the other muted white walls, green plants and soft grey carpet, the atmosphere created should have been tranquil. It wasn't. Instead it was the backdrop to many violent scenes.

I dreaded bathing when he was in the bedroom – he would lie on the bed watching me through the glass walls separating the two rooms. The glass walls built in response to his insistence. Those glass walls I had tried so hard to make brick. I wondered if he took the time to watch me deliberately. Perhaps trying to intimidate me or just to give him time to plan his next move. I wasn't allowed the space and time to get dressed while he was there. His sexual demands had to be met first. No matter the time of day or what would be happening next. I had learned that it was easier to submit so that I could get to the dinner with friends, talk I was giving or church service we were going to. It was that or a row and probably not going at all. The sex would still happen, it always did. On his terms.

There were other times when I was already half dressed and running late. Feeling frazzled. Juggling a full time job, four children and a home wasn't always plain sailing. It was then I'd react before thinking through the consequences. Move away from his advances. Turn my face the other way. Take a step in the opposite direction. Ignore him. Continue dressing. This was but for a few minutes. His hand on my jaw, sharply turning my face to look into his angry eyes, would bring me back to my reality. A barrage of sharp words accompanied his movements. "Who do you think you are? It's either willingly or I'll make you. I'll crush you into fine powder and you will be the woman you're supposed to be. Don't defy me!" There was no escape. I had my life but on his terms.

Even those times were easier to bear than some of the others. There were other times that even many years later were difficult to share. That time when I'd not wanted sex but decided to submit only to find that wasn't enough this time. This time he didn't want to see my face. He wanted a hole. His mouth screwed up into a nasty grimace, he made his demands known. A hole and nothing more. I was to stand naked, leaning forward over a bedroom arm chair. He pushed the back of my head away from him as I cried, asking him not to do this, not to treat me like this. He was caught up in the act, the moment. I was nothing to him. My voice, my cries, my pain, my brokenness was not heard. When all was done, he collapsed on the bed and slept. I finished dressing, quietly did my make up and left for work.

Later that night, he insisted he needed his "sleeping pill" – he often couldn't sleep without first having sex. I knew better than to argue. I didn't want a repeat of that morning. I submitted. I allowed my body to be used. I was learning to separate myself from what was happening. I would never survive if I continued to feel everything so acutely. So I distanced myself. I watched from the outside, aloof, looking in. Soon he would sleep and I too would sleep. Gratefully, I always slept very deeply. But he didn't drop off straight away. He knelt on the bed, took his dressing gown belt in one hand and asked me to kneel too. He pulled me closer to him and drew the soft belt loosely around us both, tying it in a knot at the ends. He then had us both lie down. He started sobbing, asking me to forgive him, repeatedly saying we were meant to be together, he loved me. I soothed him, reassured him, comforted him. Then we slept.

A few nights later I denied his demand for sex as I was menstruating. The counsellor had said I needed to train him and I should start by not agreeing to sex when I was having a period. So, in spite of the insults and hurtful things he said, I continued to say no. At one point he formed a fist and massaged it into my face while telling me what he could do to me for saying no. I was the one in the wrong. He had a right to sex. I was his wife. Although terrified and exhausted, I didn't relent.

He took his hunting knife out of a drawer and put it under his bed. If I wouldn't have sex with him, I would wake up in the morning and the children would be dead. It would be my fault. I was driving him to it. He would kill them and then himself and I would have to live with the guilt for the rest of my life.

I wrestled with my thoughts. What if he did it? Or perhaps, in the middle of the night, he would change his mind and just kill me instead. What should I do? I turned on my side away from him and prayed. I asked for protection for me and for the children. Almost immediately I saw angels. At the bottom of the bed there were four rows of angels, four in each row, facing me. They were on their haunches and they each had a sword in one hand. I could see they were waiting for something. Right next to me there was another angel. He was standing up straight, his sword in his hand. He had his back to the wall and was facing the angels at the bottom of the bed. I knew instinctively he was in charge. I knew they were waiting for his command and then they would fly into action! I was protected! My children were protected! I closed my eyes and went to sleep.

"All healing is first a healing of the heart."[5]

Carl Townsend

For me, healing is an ongoing journey. While I was contained within that abusive marriage, I used lots of different coping strategies that made me feel like I was surviving and keeping part of me intact. These did work to some degree – they enabled me to live a life that appeared reasonably normal from the outside for many years. However, they didn't prevent me from becoming more and more damaged on the inside although I didn't properly realise this while it was happening.

One of the main reasons for making the enormous decision to escape from this relationship was that I was slowly becoming increasingly aware of the detrimental effects I was experiencing. I carried an internal emotional feeling of hurt which manifested physically in my chest almost all the time as pain. I was distancing myself more and more from even everyday conversations at home. I could sense myself withdrawing into

5. Breaking the Chains in Pursuit of Healing: Breaking the Chains that Prevent Healing, Carl Townsend, 2003, Universe Publishing.

myself and this was not like me at all. I am an extrovert who loves conversation and discussion and the company of people. I found myself walking and moving slowly and deliberately as if my feet and legs were heavy – again not at all like me, as I would usually have run everywhere if I could. I was eating almost nothing and losing a lot of weight. He had said he would grind me into fine powder and he was succeeding. Together with the effect his mood swings were having on the children and his insistence on bringing another woman into the house to live with us, my own mental, emotional and physical well-being was slipping and so I decided I had to leave.

The healing process for me started with weekly counselling sessions with the Dean of Students at the Bible School I had attended. I met with him weekly for six months and then monthly for a further three. Those sessions really helped to redress the faulty thinking I had about myself and who I was. He worked with me on identifying where this had all started and why I had lived with the abuse for so many years. I am quite an analytical person so I found this to be very helpful.

My emotions, however, were still very raw. It felt like I had pieces of my soul torn away – the emotional pain was searing. Father God used other ways to start healing my soul. One evening I was in church on my own, with my children being looked after by a babysitter. I don't remember the sermon but I do remember the worship time. I was part of a very large church and we had a full band on stage leading worship. I was engaging as fully as I could, focusing all my attention on Jesus and all he had done for me. As I did so, I started seeing pictures in my mind's eye – in just a few seconds I would see a picture of me being abused and then immediately Jesus on the cross. Then another picture where I was being mistreated and misused, then the face of Jesus smiling lovingly at me. This went on a for a while, with me seeing about twelve to fifteen flash backs and each time then seeing Jesus exuding love and compassion. At the end of that time of worship I was on the floor, having poured out my heart in tears but now quiet and still. By the time I stood up, the pain in my chest had lifted. I had experienced some accelerated emotional healing.

A few years later, I dreamed that I was wearing a loose fitting dress and something was bundled inside it. I put my hand down the front of it and started pulling out lots of home-made cloth bandages which had blood on them. At this time of my life I was married to a wonderfully loving and caring man but, even so, I knew this dream was significant. I understood almost immediately that I still had stuff to deal with. I may have covered the hurt with some of my own coping strategies but I was still bleeding. After some research I found a retreat where two amazing ladies spent a number of hours praying with me. Together we asked Father God to show us what needed to be healed. He showed me that I was struggling with the demands of a full time job, four children and a new husband who seemed to expect fully cooked meals every evening. I had interpreted his expectations as demands that had to be met at all costs, no questions asked, instead of talking about what I could and could not do and even asking for help. I was pushing myself to the edge and coming undone. Once I realised that I was no longer living under a tyrant but a man of grace, I let go and the Holy Spirit came and brought healing and further freedom.

There were other times when I would be reading parts of the Bible and it would feel like a soft, warm, gentle cloud of comfort would settle on me. I would find myself at peace with the world and with God experiencing a sense of well-being and wholeness, content to be just where I was in that moment. These were moments of further healing and comfort to my soul.

Although I almost never experience flashbacks anymore, there were times when this would happen in the most ordinary and unexpected places, like washing the kitchen floor. My response to these unwelcome flashback intruders is to stop what I am doing for a moment, give them to Jesus, thank him for my freedom and that I am a daughter that he loves and delights in and then finish my task. I have found that living a normal life, without abuse and the stress and anxiety that this brings, is itself part of the healing process. Finding enjoyment and expressing gratitude for everyday things is an important aide to living in freedom.

Our Father God will use everything and anything to create healing in us. He knows us so well and wants us to live at peace with ourselves and others. I've mentioned a few of the ways he has brought healing to me and he continues to bring me into an ever increasing place of wholeness. I find it's important to be open and willing to engage with the Holy Spirit as he works with us and in us. It is, after all, for freedom that Christ Jesus has set us free.

Pause and Reflect

For all of us healing and freedom is an ongoing life long journey. This is particularly true for those of us who have experienced abuse and misuse. It takes great courage to intentionally throw yourself into healing, as there is always the lurking threat of being misunderstood and rejected but the rewards are great – a life lived without restraints: Godly freedom, peace and well-being.

1. Personally, I found counselling so helpful and I would always recommend that anyone who has experienced abuse engage in some sort of talking therapy with a qualified Christian therapist (acc-uk.org). It's a bold step

and counselling can be painful, I can't deny that, but it will help you uncover hurts that need to be faced in order to bring about your healing. Prayerfully consider if this is something you could benefit from.

2. Do you suffer with flashbacks? Sometimes these can help you identify something that is unresolved and some prayer ministry could help with that. Is there anyone you can ask to pray with you? Perhaps a Sozo session would help (bethelsozo.org.uk).

3. If you're struggling with nightmares, come before God in prayer, perhaps with a prayer partner. Ask God to fill your mind with good things and settle your soul in peaceful sleep. As you're falling asleep, remind yourself of all the things you're grateful for. Do this every evening before falling asleep.

4. Fill yourself with the promises of God for your life. This could be ones you've received through prophetic words spoken over you or those you've read in the Bible. The words we read are often like cool, cleansing water washing over our souls.

5. Be bold and ask our Father God to accelerate your healing – and see what he will do for you!

CHAPTER SIX

Unrestrained – Reach out to Others

The counsellor's words punched me in the stomach. Seeing the colour drain from my face, he repeated some of what he had just told me. He had had a visitor last night. It was my husband. He had persistently and annoyingly pushed the button on the intercom at the gate of their property, even when the counsellor had told him to come and see him in the office the following morning. Eventually the counsellor had walked down the drive and met him at the gate. Fortunately, this was some distance from the rest of his house where his wife and adult children were enjoying a peaceful evening outside in the garden, watching the sun as it retreated behind a haze of orange tinted clouds on the horizon, their small dogs resting at his wife's feet.

As the counsellor opened the gate to speak to him face to face, he became aware of a black pistol in his hand draped at his side. Fortunately, he wasn't threatening him or brandishing the pistol about but nonetheless its presence caused the counsellor tension belied by the calm tone he used to ask him what he could do for him that couldn't wait until the morning. Wisely, he chose to ignore the presence of the pistol and engaged further in as normal a conversation as possible. Rather than anger and aggression, the replies the counsellor received revealed a measure of anguish and self-pity. He was struggling. Nothing was changing. In fact, it was getting worse. I was getting worse. I was becoming less submissive. He was getting less sex. He cried. His life wasn't worth living like this. He wanted to end it all. Lifting the pistol to his chest, he explained that he had a licence for it. He could use it on himself in some lane where no-one would hear him. The only thing stopping him was the thought of the children – he would miss them.

Although I wasn't aware that he had this pistol (he had sold the one I knew about some years before), the story of suicidal thoughts was one that I had become familiar with recently. On one afternoon, while we were in the car without the children and he was driving, we had drifted into an intense, painful conversation where I had held my ground. My stance was more than he could bear. Blaming me for his dissatisfaction with the state of his life, he had threatened to drive the car into a number of different trees as we drove up to and then past them. He felt his life was over and that he couldn't live without getting what he wanted, how he wanted it and when he wanted it. He told me he often felt like just crashing into a telephone pole or tree and ending his life when he was driving alone but, in fact, this would be better if both of us died together as this really was all my fault anyway. I felt fear rising inside me and quickly decided to push these feelings down, to tuck them away deep inside me so I could deal with them at another time. I needed to stay clearheaded and devise a way of calming him down. Painting a picture of what life would be like for the children without us – how much they would miss us, we wouldn't be able to protect them, where would they live, how they wouldn't cope – seemed to settle him a little. Enough to get us home safely.

The counsellor was encouraging me to make sure I was keeping myself and the children safe. He knew it was difficult and said it would be extremely challenging for anyone. I was encouraged to keep hoping for a good outcome. An outcome where my marriage was saved and the children could grow up in a peaceful environment. He wanted to identify a prayer partner for me – someone I could meet with weekly – and would give this some thought. In the meantime, it was Chapel Time for the Church Staff and he felt it would be good for me to join him there.

Chapel started with worship. I drank in the healing presence of God and allowed my heart to cry out, hope against hope. I asked Father God to show me my husband as he saw him. Almost immediately I saw a picture of him in the middle of our bedroom on his own. He stood with his head held back and his face turned upwards towards the ceiling, his legs spread out wider than his hips. Within seconds it seemed he was being pulled by each arm in different directions. His face contorted into various expressions, mostly anguish. He was being flung from one end of the room to the other relentlessly. I started praying for him. For peace to come on him and in him. It was clear to me that he was being tormented. I cried out for release for him. For victory over this oppression. For joy to come.

As Chapel came to an end and we were leaving, the counsellor introduced me to one of the pastor's wives. She had agreed to be my prayer partner for a while. We exchanged contact details and set up a time to meet in a week's time. Feeling cared for and supported, I walked back to my car. A sense of renewed hope seemed to have taken root, especially because of what God had shown me. Perhaps he could be set free. Maybe prayer and fasting would mean that demonic strongholds would be relinquished. It wasn't over yet.

"No one is useless in this world who lightens the burdens of another."[6]

Charles Dickens

I am so grateful to God that he has placed people in my life from time to time who have loved and cared for me. When I was a child it was an older couple, friends of my parents, who paid me attention and bought me treats from time to time. Mostly though, the church became my place of safety and care. My younger sisters and I were picked up from home each Sunday for Sunday School and church and then dropped off again. We learnt Bible verses each week and received beautiful stickers when we got them right. Eventually I became part of the children's choir and donned specially made red capes each time we sang for the growing congregation. On really special occasions, such as the opening of the new church building, I sang a solo and my parents came along too. I even had my photo in the local newspaper! Our pastor always did a short piece directly aimed at the children during the main service before we went off for our Sunday School classes. It was usually interactive – I often answered questions and offered up my opinions. I felt I belonged here.

I was married in a different church, one I attended with my husband-to-be, and we continued to attend church throughout our marriage. It was a vibrant, growing church in a small town with lots of young couples and families. I had friends there but none I confided in. Later on, some of these friends told me they suspected something wasn't right and could see I was always trying to make sure he was happy. He was known to

---

6. Doctor Marigold, Charles Dickens, 2013, A Word to the Wise Publishers.

be a bit of an awkward man with strong opinions but he was also charming at times and usually gave generously into the work of the church. Personally, I preferred to keep what was happening at home separate from my life at church. This was a place where I could be a different person and step into roles and jobs that helped me to feel more whole and worthwhile.

We moved away from this town and church during the final year of Bible School and became members of the church that hosted the Bible School. As mentioned above, as part of the counselling I received, I was also offered other support, including the prayer partner organised for me. I met with her weekly and told her what was happening at home. She listened and didn't hide her emotional responses. She gave me practical advice. In reality, this was the first time anyone had so clearly and outrightly told me that what I was experiencing wasn't right. She gave me examples from her own life and marriage that contrasted starkly with what I was going through. She explicitly told me that I should not put up with it. That I should leave. That I was not safe.

I also spoke on the phone to a very dear older Christian friend of mine on an almost daily basis during this time. I had known her for many years and respected her as a woman of God who embodied humility and a close walk with Father God. Previously, I had not confided in her about the abuse in my marriage but at this time I felt I needed covering in prayer. I knew she loved me as one of her own children and even spoke of me as her eldest child (she had three other children). I am convinced that her prayers during the months leading up to and during the separation, divorce and moving overseas protected me from more serious harm. During our almost daily conversations she encouraged me to keep myself and the children safe. She alerted me to potentially dangerous situations that I hadn't seen. She made sure I had put practical things in place and asked me questions so that I would think things through carefully. Mostly, she encouraged me to leave. She helped me to see that the marriage I was in was not a healthy one and may never be so without radical change – and there was no evidence that this change was happening.

I am also forever grateful for the nine months of counselling I received once I had separated from him and was living on my own with the children. Especially because it was given free of charge. I could never have afforded it otherwise. On one occasion, the counsellor gave me money and told me to buy vitamins – I was looking worn out and ill. Small kindnesses like this touched my heart and made me feel valued.

Once I had left him, I started going to a church midweek small group held in a home. I knew I needed the support of a group of faith-filled friends. This group became a caring community who prayed with me through each traumatic episode and even helped with a replacement car when I had an accident, as well as gifts of money when I was struggling financially. Individually and collectively, they were an example of the love, compassion and provision of God – the church at its best. There is no better place to be than in a loving and caring church community that is committed to hearing from God and being his hands, feet and heart with those who are suffering.

Pause and Reflect

Jesus told us that we would be known by our love one for another (John 13:34-35). We were not created to do life on our own. However, if you've been cut off from your family and friends (sometimes for years) it may feel more natural to withdraw from people, away from eyes that may see the anguish in your heart. It is often one of the tactics an abuser uses – separating the abused person from any sort of supportive relationships. Or you may have trusted someone with the story of what was happening to you only to be ridiculed, gossiped about or cast aside. It may be that you haven't experienced the sincere loving kindness of people for years or even ever. I have good news for you: there are people who Father God is putting into your life right now to love and care for you. They may not be obvious to you at this exact moment but they are there. How do I know that? Because our loving heavenly Father God wouldn't tell us over and over again to love one another (1 Peter 1:22) without providing a loving, nurturing environment for you to heal in – filled with people who will look out for you and love you. Perhaps you just need a little help identifying them.

1. Jot down the names of people you see on a regular basis. These may just be casual friends or acquaintances or they may be family and close friends. Make a list of as many as you can think of. Don't leave them off the list just because you're younger or older than they are. Include everyone you can think of. Now circle those you feel some affinity with – even if you don't know them very well. Those you think you could enjoy having a coffee with (or peppermint tea, in my case).

2. Next, make a list of people you don't see all the time but do have some contact with, perhaps through social media, Whatsapp or text. Again, circle those you would love to have a coffee with if they lived closer to you.

3. If you're a church goer, find out if there are any midweek small group meetings you could join. It can be quite scary to join a group and be the newbie but most small groups are used to inviting new people into the group. Or go to one that a friend or acquaintance goes to so you

know at least one person right away. That group may be exactly what you need – people who will look out for you.

4. If you go to a church that prays for people at the end of Sunday services, go forward and be prayed for as often as you want to. Refuse to accept the lie in your head that the thing you are struggling with is not worth someone else's prayers! If your church doesn't offer this on Sundays, do you know anyone you could ask to pray with you every now and again. Fifteen minutes of God-empowered prayer can make such a difference. On TSM (tsmbedford.org) we have a saying, "God can do a lot in 10 minutes."

5. Have you thought about getting some counselling? Is there someone in your own church who may be able to offer this to you? Or perhaps they can put you in contact with someone who can? Talking things through with someone who has your best interests at heart is one of the best things you can do for yourself.

Now look back at your responses. Have you identified people you could have some coffee with and so develop a friendship? Are there one or two (maybe more) you feel you could share your heart with and still feel accepted and valued? If not, maybe that will come in time as you reach out to others. Could you join a small group? Can you find a way to get prayer now and again or more often? What about the possibility of counselling – what could be your first step?

CHAPTER SEVEN

Unrestrained – Deal with Disappointment

The natural pool of water in front of me was bordered by green leafy plants, some with long tapering leaves, others wide and flat. I could hear the soft sounds of birds gently moving into position on branches in tall trees a few metres away. The sun was warm upon my bare arms as I sat on a wooden bench allowing myself a peaceful moment – or at least a moment of inactivity. I should have been experiencing contentment and quiet joy in order to be truly part of this serene scene. Outwardly, to any passer-by, it would have looked as though I was indeed at peace with the world.

However, the opposite was true: I was in turmoil. I had reached a point of no return. A decision needed to be made and only I could make it. A decision I knew I would not reverse. It had taken me a very long time to come to this point. I had agonised over it. I had fought against making my children or myself a statistic. Children from a "broken home". Me, a divorced woman. It felt more like a "broken woman" and children "divorced" from their father. I hated the idea. But I just could not go on any longer. I was feeling increasingly brutalised, crushed and destroyed. I lifted my eyes from the water towards the counsellor's office and then trudged slowly in that direction, anxiety leaden in my stomach.

He greeted me in his usual friendly manner but, sensing I was ill at ease, immediately asked some searching questions. Hesitantly, I was able to bring into the open my desire to leave. Expecting resistance, I spoke carefully and slowly. I really didn't have the emotional energy for a confrontation – even only a verbal one. It was known that this counsellor, in fact the church's stance, was always to keep husbands and wives together. Separation and divorce were the very last, very extreme solution for only those couples who were, in a nutshell, "too bound up in their own selfishness to be willing to make the changes necessary to preserve their relationship". Thus, I expected the worse. Presenting a defence for myself and my own predicament would be necessary but I was worn out and exhausted. Faltering over my words, hesitant and near tears, I tried.

The counsellor responded with unanticipated compassion. He used picture language to sketch a scene. Describing a house that was on fire and burning and then a person who had managed to get out not only by themselves but with the children they loved and cared for, he asked if I thought anyone would force this person to go back into the house while the fire raged? Would any observer judge or condemn the person for escaping this blaze? What did I think would be the right reaction to such a person? He waited for the full impact of what he was saying to become part of my conscious thinking. I could leave without shame or blame.

Continuing, he acknowledged that, if it were possible, he would like to put me in a state of stasis, frozen perhaps, while my husband had time to change and then I could be unfrozen at the right time. As this was not humanly possible, he understood that I had come to the conclusion that this was as far as I could go at the moment and therefore I needed to leave. An uneasiness began to rise in the pit of my stomach again. I wasn't sure that he realised I would not be going back – ever. It seemed as if he held out a measure of hope that there would be substantial change and we could be reconciled, but I did not have the emotional capacity to embrace that idea. For years, I had nurtured faith for significant change but the reserves of faith and hope I had left were for my future. I wanted to direct these into starting my adult life over again from scratch on my own with my children. I voiced my concerns. He admitted that only thirty percent of those couples who separated ever reconciled, meaning seventy percent never did. He was being realistic.

Our time wasn't over yet. I didn't want to disappoint my Father God. Didn't the Bible say that God hated divorce? Wouldn't God judge me and find me wanting? Had I really tried hard enough to make this marriage work? Perhaps it was selfishness that was driving me to leave? Could I live a life knowing that God may never give me space to speak, teach, preach or lead in the church again? After all, I would be a divorced woman. This counsellor listened to my questions, my tearful ramblings. My disappointment in myself was evident. He then prayed God's peace, comfort and love over me and over my children. He prayed words of strength and courage for this next part of my journey. As he was praying, God showed him a picture. He was sitting with a group of male leaders in the church, and from other churches, around his large board room table. They were discussing operational and strategic issues pertinent to the Kingdom of God. And on one of the chairs, engrossed in the conversations and decisions being made, was me. God was saying he had not discounted me. My circumstances had not discounted me. Others would not discount me. He would give me a place at the table of ministry. My heart was encouraged. My Father God still had a future and a hope for me. I was not to be marginalised or sidelined. I was still his daughter. A daughter with purpose.

"Don't let today's disappointments cast a shadow on tomorrow's dreams."[7]

Unknown

I had entered this marriage as a young woman with so many expectations and hopes. I had expected to be loved, cared for, nurtured even. I thought I would settle into a marriage where our shared values were lived out together. I would have children, own a house, have a good job, enjoy church, laugh a lot. In truth, some of my expectations were based on romantic nonsense – mainly because of the number of historical romantic novels I had read in my teenage years. I realised I would almost certainly find life different from that experienced by many of my heroines but I hadn't realised to what extent. I have heard it said that disappointment is what we experience as a result of the distance between our expectations and actual reality – I found this to be true.

Before you can actually deal with disappointment, you have to recognise you are experiencing the negative effects of it. Part of being human means most of us won't change the

---

7. https://worldfactsbook.com/dont-let-todays-disappointments-cast-a-shadow-on-tomorrows-dreams/

things we are comfortable with. It took me a long time to realise that I was disappointed with how my life was playing out. I had become adept at managing my circumstances and my emotions. I had lowered my expectations in an effort to minimise the sense of loss and hurt I felt. In the back of my mind, I knew I wanted my life to be different but I couldn't see a way out that lined up with my values and how I thought I would be perceived by others. I wanted so much to do the right thing in the eyes of church leaders and in the eyes of God. So I convinced myself that I could live a full life, which was acceptable, if I expected less.

Looking back, I realised I was believing lies about so many things and in particular how Father God saw me and expected me to behave. It wasn't until some years later that I looked disappointment square in the eyes though.

I had just heard the news, via a telephone call, that the children's father had died during the night. At the time of this news we had been divorced for many years. I had remarried and was living in a different country. It wasn't a shock, as we knew he had cancer and was in hospital. After comforting the children, I took a shower. Suddenly, I found myself weeping uncontrollably. Wave after wave of disappointment welled up within me and spilled over in tears. I cried out loud for all the wasted years, wasted opportunities. I remembered a dream God had given him in the early years of our marriage where he had been taking truck loads of leather shoes into areas of extreme poverty throughout Africa. None of it had come into being. As I cried, I realised that so much had been lost, now without any hope of it ever becoming a reality. Our Father God had had wonderful partnership plans for him, all now lost, never to be retrieved.

I had not expected to cry and had no idea I would experience any sense of loss at his death. I was also surprised at how disappointment had come rushing out of me. Right where I was, I started talking to Father God about how I felt about all those wasted years. How it was unfair that I needed to lower and even give up expectations I had held. It seemed I had become less of a person then – I had limited myself to what I could see would work. Joy had all but disappeared. My world had become smaller then. At the time I hadn't seen this. But right then, years later, I could see my life had been contained and constrained by what I thought was living in the reality of my circumstances.

For me, that moment with Father God in the shower was a defining one. I repented of hemming myself in, lowering my expectations of life and all God could and would do. Already I had started to see glimpses of the plans that God might have for me. Right then these glimpses expanded: I experienced a broadening of my horizons, a widening of the space around me, a deepening of hope. Expectations were reignited. As I pushed the walls of disappointment over, bright light dispelled the grey shadows and I believed I had a new future.

Pause and Reflect

Disappointment has a very definite restraining effect. Where you once may have reached out and grasped new opportunities, you find you feel like you are doing life with your arms tied to your sides, unable to take on anything new and exciting. Disappointment robs you of positive emotions you may have felt, such as joy and eager anticipation. However, life is full of disappointments, small and big, but the negative impact on your life can be diminished if you refuse to harbour disappointment in your heart once you're aware of it. Father God has good plans for your life – if you find that difficult to believe, it may be that disappointment is lurking in your heart. Find a quiet space and take a few moments to go through the following steps to see what God may do in and through you today.

1. Close your eyes and focus all your attention on Father God. He loves you and cares for you. He wants to spend this time with you. Enjoy recognising that he is right there, in the moment, with you.

2. Ask him to show you if there is any disappointment in your heart. Is there a sadness that comes over you when you think of what might have been in a given situation? Or perhaps anger surfaces? Or do you find yourself feeling cynical – nothing good could really happen to you?

3. Allow yourself to experience fully those emotions – these will be different for each person. Now is the time to pour out your heart – ask the questions you haven't dared to utter before. It may be that you feel let down by other people or even by God himself. It's important not to rush this part. Know that there is nothing you can say that will make God love you less. He already knows what is in your heart – let it out. Only once you've spent some time telling Father God about everything you are feeling and thinking, only then read on.

4. Some things are gone forever and cannot be restored. This could be because, for example, someone has died or an operation has taken place that cannot be reversed. Acceptance is necessary in these circumstances. The Bible speaks of being like a "weaned child" that is content (Psalm 131:2). This is a picture of a child that has been used to the comfort of breast milk and now has moved onto solid foods. The child doesn't understand why they can't have breast milk any longer and probably had a

good cry (tantrums even) through the weaning process but now lies contentedly in their mother's arms having spent all their emotions. Verse 1 speaks of not being concerned with things "too wonderful for me". We really don't understand everything that we go through – the whys and what ifs. But we can get to a place where we are like a weaned child, content in the arms of Father God, having given up our right to know why, trusting that he loves and cares for us more than we can know.

5. There are also areas in our lives that have caused disappointment that are not over forever. You may have laid down dreams and ambitions believing that you didn't have it in you ever to accomplish them. Maybe you eventually believed the lies that were being spoken over you almost daily. If that's you, let me encourage you to allow Father God to stir your heart again. Lean into him and ask him to show you how he sees you and what he sees you doing. Do that right now. Allow joy, excitement and anticipation to rise up within you again. Father God says that he will restore to you the years eaten by locusts (Joel 2:24-26). Let your heart jump for joy at the prospect of this!

6. Whether you have come to a place of quiet acceptance, having given up your right to understand, or renewed joy at the prospect of a reignited dream, now is the time to bring God praise. Worship him for who he is: a good Father, kind, full of grace and mercy, loving, generous, faithful, patient, healer and miracle worker.

CHAPTER EIGHT

Unrestrained – Hear God

I don't dream very often. They say we all dream every night but I don't usually remember my dreams. However, those I do remember are often significant. Yet I have dreamed two memorable dreams within the space of two weeks. In fact, one was more of a waking dream – I was somewhere between being awake and falling asleep but not quite there yet. That in between stage. That was an amazing dream or was it a vision? So comforting. So uplifting. However the other one came first.

I couldn't breathe. I felt like I was suffocating. I was in a large, Olympic size swimming pool, an indoors one. There were lots of people sitting around the edges of the pool watching me while I was in the water on my own. These people were mostly sitting on chairs close to the edge of the pool. A few were standing up. Then it dawned on me: these were people I knew – they were my in-laws. I had lots of in-laws: it was a big family. A number of the women were leaning forward in their chairs, blankets over their legs, cushions behind their backs, obviously comfortable. Everyone, men and women, had smiles on their faces. They were relaxed. All were looking my way but doing nothing to help me. Some were pointing towards me, laughing, taking some delight in my predicament, finding it funny. I looked around the pool, searching anxiously – wasn't there anyone in the water who could help me? I realised I was totally alone. Isolated. Underwater. My whole body was fully submerged and I was sinking. I felt heavy and numb. I couldn't feel or see the bottom of the pool. I couldn't breathe. I was suffocating. Some sort of pressure was forcing me downwards. I would die if I didn't get to the bottom of the pool quickly and shoot myself back up to the top. That is if I reached the bottom at all. I couldn't see where it was or how far I still had to go. The water was becoming increasingly murky.

Just then, I felt God speak to me, telling me to relax. To stop trying so hard. That I *could* breathe. He would make it so that I could draw air from the water – like a fish – until I reached the top again. I wouldn't die. Relieved, I felt every iota of anxiety and fear leave me. I drifted effortlessly down towards the bottom of the pool until my toes and then bottom of my feet touched the solid floor of the pool. All the while I was breathing! I was drawing in air from the water, right into my lungs! I pushed firmly against the bottom of the pool, catapulting myself upwards through the water towards the top. Calm and unhindered, my body sliced through the water, eventually reaching the surface. As my head emerged, I gasped, gulping in great swathes of air, filling every cell of my body with an abundance of life-giving oxygen. I had survived.

I woke up from the dream experiencing a mixture of emotions. Why had no one tried to help me? Were they unaware of what was happening to me? In my dream I had nearly died. I was confused but also very grateful. Father God had made it possible for my body to inhale the oxygen I needed from water. And yes, it wasn't as comfortable as breathing in fresh air but it had meant I survived! I felt soothed. I instinctively knew the significance of the dream: My life wasn't easy and it felt like it was becoming ever more challenging and even dangerous but God was with me and therefore I would get through this in one piece. I would survive!

Within days of this dream I experienced my first semi-awake dream. In bed, as I closed my eyes, I immediately saw an angel who took me by the hand. Together we floated just a few centimetres above the ground over bright, almost luminous green hills. After a while, we sat down on bright green grass near a clear water stream. Facing each other, the angel asked me a question, "What do you want?" His voice sounded like water moving over stones and rocks on a warm summer's day. "I want to know that God is with me," I answered. Instantly he took my hand and once again we glided over hills and valleys. In the distance I saw a walled city and, as we drew closer, I noticed a long road which divided the city into two halves. We travelled along this road. As we came close to reaching the end of the road, I became aware of a soft, orange-tinged, soft gold light emanating from somewhere within the city and filling every available nook and cranny as well as the atmosphere surrounding it. It was all encompassing. I knew it was where God was! Up to this point, although I felt peaceful and content, I had so many unanswered questions I wanted to ask. Not questions about this experience but questions about what I was going through. Why? When would I be free from the pain and hurt? How would that happen? What should I do? However, as I was led towards and into this light, every question disappeared! Overwhelmed by a sense of the imminent, tangible presence of God, all I wanted to do was sit and rest with him. My questions seemed not insignificant but answered without ever being uttered.

This experience instilled in me a quiet sense of confident security and peace that my soul so needed. I hadn't felt like I could walk through these days without knowing that Father God was with me and in this half-awake dream, I felt reassured that he was. I didn't have answers to my questions, at least not in actual words. Be that as it may, my heart seemed content and my mind quiet – the warm, bright light of the presence of Father God had healed the anguish of my soul and I felt strengthened enough to continue.

"We often miss hearing God's voice simply because we aren't paying attention."[8]

Rick Warren

Our God speaks to us in so very many different ways and it would take a whole separate book to properly unpack and discuss how that happens. So here I want only to share a few of my own experiences of hearing the voice of God. I've heard it said that we as Christians think that because God is unchanging, his activities are also always the same. We restrict God, in our expectations of him, to speaking and acting in those ways which are familiar to us through our own experience of him and through what we have read of him in the Bible. Our Father God will, however, use whatever means he likes to speak to us. He is the God of infinite variety!

For some of us, we don't even expect God to use methods which we have read about in the Bible. You may have immediately discounted or doubted my experiences of angels and yet there are numerous accounts of God speaking to

---

8. Can you hear me now? Rick Warren, Audio series at https://store.pastorrick.com/can-you-hear-me-now-complete-audio-series.html

people through dreams of angels (Matthew 1:20; 2:13) and the physical presence of angels (Luke 1:26-38; 2: 8-14). Even in the Old Testament some saw angels (Judges 6: 11-22; 1 Kings 19: 5-9). Why would our loving heavenly Father not send angels to serve us too at times (Hebrews 1:14)? My mother was not a Christian when she became pregnant with me as a teenager. She knew only of God through the life and testimony of one of her grandmothers, who she remembers saw a vision of heaven as she was dying. Being quite distressed at being pregnant with me at not quite sixteen years of age, my mother cried out to God to show himself to her. In the middle of the night she woke up and saw a shining being sitting on her radiator with a large book open on his lap. His eyes seemed to be following his finger as he looked for something in the book and then he stopped, closed the book, got up, laid his hand on her stomach and then disappeared. My mother believes he blessed her and me, even though it would be many years before she became a Christ follower herself and I was, at that stage, unborn.

Most of the time I hear the voice of God in two ways: reading the Bible and a quiet voice on the inside of me. There are moments when that voice is louder and clearer but mostly it's very gentle. When we were considering whether we should move to Bedford or commute to church from Peterborough where we lived, we were asking God to speak to us. After some soul searching, we thought God didn't mind and it wouldn't matter. So we decided to commute. We had a lovely house and children and grandchildren in Peterborough so it made more sense to do so. Literally within minutes of this decision being made during a handsfree telephone discussion while driving, I clearly heard a few sentences in my mind: "Move to Bedford. I've got a plan for how you will see your family in Peterborough." It was so clear, I was immediately in tears and had to pull over. We put our house on the market and it sold within twenty-four hours.

Other times, the voice of God is almost inaudible and I find it can be crowded out by the other voices and sounds in my life. I am getting better at recognising his gentle promptings but I still find myself repenting as I make mistakes and don't take time to hear him. I love the Bible and the way Father God uses it. When I'm reading the Bible, verses or phrases may speak to my situation or challenge me in a particular way. I remember once feeling really quite ill and weak. I had a virus and it was taking a long time for me to get better. As I sat and read the Word one day, I physically felt strength return to my body. I felt nourished and made sudden, good progress. It was as if the written word of God had physically nourished my body while I was reading it!

I'm quite a visual person and I find that Father God shows me things in pictures at times. I could be on the streets or in church and I will see in my mind's eye a part of a body that needs healing. Sometimes I know who that is for but often I don't. It's a journey in learning to partner with God who chooses to make us his hands, feet and voice. Or as I'm praying for someone, I see situations or scenarios and then pray into those. I almost always ask the person if what I saw or prayed for made sense and how. I love it when what I've seen or heard is right and people feel loved by Father God as a result. If it's not quite right, that's fine too – I'm still learning to recognise the voice of God and loving the adventure of it.

I know God speaks to both Christians and those who don't know him yet through dreams too. Some have seen a man in white and searched for him, not realising it was Jesus appearing to them in a dream. How amazing is that! I have found that Father God uses dreams to warn me of enemy activity at times. The swimming bath dream above was one such dream. Life was going to get even tougher and God was preparing me by affirming that I would be OK. The half-awake dream above brought me to a place of deep gratitude for the comfort of his presence and love for me and this helped to sustain me during the months ahead.

Sometimes Father God will use the wise words of others to help us. These may be the words of a friend directly talking us through a problem or unintentionally mentioning something that we find helpful or that leads to a powerful lightbulb moment. Or you may, as I often do, find wisdom in something you read or a song you hear or sing. Father God will use whatever he can to bring you freedom!

Our loving Father God wants to speak to us as any good parent would want to communicate with their child. It's up to us to open our hearts and minds and submit ourselves to his voice and promptings.

Pause and Reflect

How does God speak to you? When are you most likely to hear him? Where would you be? What time of day? Do you need to be on your own or with others? Does listening to worship music help you hear God's voice or is a walk in a forest better for you?

1. Have a think about when you hear Father God speaking to you. Remember that often his is a quiet voice rather than a megaphone! Remember a time when you felt his promptings, experienced his comfort or heard his directive words. Describe what you were doing at the time. Think about the time of day and whether you were with anyone else. This will help you to discover

when you are most likely to hear his voice for yourself. Then you can make sure you create circumstances that help you to hear what he wants to say to you on a more regular basis. This can only be good!

2. Expect God to speak to you in unexpected ways. It may be that you are watching a movie and the plotline gives you insight into something you are finding challenging. Maybe a line in a novel you are reading jumps out at you. Perhaps you are digging up weeds or eating fruit cake and you feel God speaking to you. Our Father God will use all sorts of things and situations, sounds and smells even, to communicate with us!

3. Would you like Father God to speak to you in dreams and visions? Ask him to! He has made a promise that this can happen:

Joel 2:28-29

And afterward,
I will pour out my Spirit on all people.
Your sons and daughters will prophesy,
your old men will dream dreams,
your young men will see visions.
Even on my servants, both men and women,
I will pour out my Spirit in those days.

CHAPTER NINE

Unrestrained – Reclaim your Uniqueness

Right there in front of me was the answer to a prayer I had prayed just a few days ago. A notice about a fully furnished house immediately available for rent, not too far away. The children wouldn't have to move schools or nursery. I could stay in my job too. I wrote down the number and called to arrange a viewing. It had everything the children and I needed. An extra room meant I could even take a lodger if I needed to. I wasn't sure how I could leave without undergoing serious harm but I did know God was with me.

The evening had degenerated into verbal attacks and blaming. Behind our closed bedroom door, I allowed insult after insult to mix with the air above my head, keeping my thoughts busy with other observations so that these daggers could not take root in my heart. This strategy was only partially successful as the words were heard – they did travel through my ears and into my mind. I was a terrible mother. I had never been able to create a home. I didn't know what a wife should be like. I would never make anyone happy. I was rebellious and rebellion was like witchcraft. I did the devil's work for him. I needed to be remade. I was holding him back.

It was his right to have someone else in the house who knew how to be a good wife. With total resignation, I didn't retaliate or defend myself. I couldn't muster any desire to fight back. It just had to end.

As he paused momentarily, I quietly uttered a few short sentences, "I'll leave. With the children. You can start again." He stopped speaking, caught off guard I suspected. "I won't go far. I'll live in a furnished house close by so you can see the children. Then you can bring who you like into this house." I had given in. He had got what he wanted – almost. I explained that two women in the house would confuse the children and that wouldn't be fair to them. He sat down in the bedroom arm chair, seemingly at a loss for words. Within a few seconds he lifted his head and the relief was visible. We agreed to speak to the children in the morning.

The four children sat on the long sofa opposite us. We had agreed the words and phrases we would use to explain what was going to happen in the next few days. The children shifted around on the sofa, with the girls doing most of the wriggling. He told them off, sternly. They sat still. He'd insisted on doing the talking. Regardless of our conversation earlier that morning, he plunged in immediately telling them that I was at fault. It was my idea to take them away. One of the twins started giggling – she always did when she was nervous. He jumped up, grasped her arm and shouted at her. I quickly intervened, explaining her nervousness. He sat back down. He told them he loved them and would see them all the time and then he got up, walked out of the room and said he was going for a drive.

The children gathered round me while I explained with as little emotion as I could that we would be moving the next day and needed to pack our clothes. The boys had questions about school and friends and when they would see their father. I answered all in as much detail as I could. We spent the rest of the morning packing clothes, toys and books. Although we weren't going to be very far away, I knew it could be difficult to come back to fetch anything. The house we were going to was furnished so we didn't need to take too much.

He didn't come home again until the following morning and that was only to shower and change. The children weren't up yet. As he was leaving, he called back to me saying I should make sure I was gone by the time he arrived home later that day. Once the children were up and dressed and had eaten breakfast, we loaded the car and drove to our new home. It took two trips and then we had everything we needed in the new spaces. I had left the new address on a piece of paper on the kitchen worktop so that he knew where the children were.

We didn't hear from him for about three days. My eldest son seemed to be struggling the most and was unable to make even small decisions. When asked to bring me a spoon, he came back with nothing, not being able to decide between various spoons. Once I realised this, we had a chat about what was happening in our lives. Uncertainty and insecurity were affecting him. He wasn't sure if we were going to return in a few days' time. I explained that we were not going back at all and he started to settle and become himself again.

A knocking sound at my bedroom window woke me up one night. Pulling the curtains back, I realised it was him and he was drunk. He wanted to see the children. I told him to leave and come back in the morning when he was sober. He started shouting at me and so I told him I would call the police if he didn't leave. He didn't leave and the police arrived but by this time he was nowhere to be found. When he arrived the next day, he told me he had been sitting in a tree watching as the police looked around in the dark for him. He also said he wanted us home and that he had made a mistake. Thus, a new struggle began.

"Don't undermine your worth by comparing yourself with others. It is because we are different that each of us is special."[9]

Brian Dyson

I have always considered myself to be someone who has never been jealous of anyone else. I have had friends over the years who have really struggled with deeply desiring what others had: attractiveness, kindness or success. I didn't feel that way. I genuinely wished people well and encouraged them to be everything they could be. I didn't experience feelings of jealousy or envy almost ever, really.

However, this didn't mean that I never compared myself to others. I did. All the time. At the core of my being I wanted to be what I considered to be normal. I wanted a normal life with normal relationships and normal things. As a child I always felt like everyone could see that we often didn't have enough of most things at home. Biscuits, cheese and lemonade were strictly rationed and kept for my dad's packed work lunches in the main. By the end of the month we often didn't have enough money to buy bread for sandwiches. My clothes were

9. Speech given by former CEO of Coca-Cola Enterprises, Brian Dyson. https://language. chinadaily.com.cn/2006-03/13/content_533554.htm

hand-me-downs from others or made by my mother. I almost always felt I was less than others but, more than this, I wanted normal relationships. Desperately. I did feel loved in rare moments. I can remember my dad taking me out of the bath once, wrapping a towel around me and patting my hair dry. This was not a usual occurrence and I felt loved and treasured. When Dad very occasionally dried or brushed my hair, he did so tentatively, with gentleness, trying not to pull or yank my head. I loved it. I also knew that he thought I was clever. He would, ever so rarely, do a bit of homework with me, especially maths. He expected a lot of me and I remember him asking what had happened to the other four percent when I got ninety-six percent for a maths test. Yes, I was a bit deflated by this but I also deep down knew he loved me. This was what I wanted – a loving family. This was what I believed to be a normal life.

That sense of safety and security was what I craved throughout childhood and my abusive marriage. I saw it in the lives of others and I desired it, intensely. I felt a very real lack of it. I wanted a stable, strong base. I could see the signs in the marriages of my friends of an intimacy that seemed able to withstand the effects of arguments and differences of opinion – and I wanted that. The reality was that I lived with a heightened sense of anxiety and alertness, always trying to avert confrontation before it happened or endeavouring to preserve the façade of all being well.

I now recognise that comparing my life with that of others was probably a natural by-product of the abuse I was suffering. It didn't spill over into jealousy or envy in my case but I have seen people become very vindictive as a result of the helplessness they feel to change their situations. Others feel overcome by both helplessness and a pervading sense of increasing hopelessness and turn these feelings inwards. This can manifest itself as self-harm and even attempts at suicide.

Many years after I had left that abusive marriage, I found myself still comparing myself and my life with that of others. I hadn't recognised it as something that was affecting my life negatively at all, as I wasn't experiencing any powerful emotions that I could associate with this ongoing comparison. I am grateful that Father God does not expect us to sort everything out all at once. It was during the Training for Supernatural Ministry course I mentioned earlier (tsmbedford.org) at the Kings Arms Church that I experienced some freedom in this area of my life. I decided from the beginning that I would throw myself into it wholeheartedly and embrace all that Father God had for me during the year of the course. What I didn't realise was that much of the first term (and some after that) was based on discovering and strengthening your identity as a child of a loving Father God. Very early on I became aware that I thought Father God was a bit ashamed of me. That he didn't want to put me on show – he wanted me to be effective in his kingdom but in the background and out of sight. I was damaged goods and my own decisions and sin had put me in harm's way. He loved me but he was not proud of me in the way that a loving parent delights in the accomplishments of a child, asking them to perform for others, displaying their talents. No, he loved me but preferred to keep me hidden.

Up to this point in my journey with God I had not realised I felt or thought this but I did. This was my way of making sense of why my life compared so unfavourably with those of others. It was distorted thinking. I had to deal with the lie I was believing about myself and the lie that I was believing about the character and nature of Father God. I acknowledged that I felt inadequate, contained, squashed, unappreciated, undervalued and that I believed Father God capable of feeling ashamed of me. The pain of this went deep and I sobbed as I allowed it to fill me. I am so grateful that I am aware that I am capable of such distorted thinking – so grateful that Father God brought what I believed of him out of a dark place into a place where I could look at the lie and see it for what it was.

Our Father God delights in each of us. He loves it when we obediently take a step into the spotlight and when we encourage others to do so too. He's not into keeping any of us in hiding! I fully believe I don't need to compare my life, who I am and what Father God is doing with me, with anyone else's journey. However, sometimes I still catch myself doing so. In fact, sometimes I now experience feelings of hurt when I see someone else's success. This may not sound like progress but it is. Numbed and thwarted emotional responses can't be acknowledged or dealt with. For me, freedom comes when I move out in obedience and speak words of encouragement and congratulation to and over the person whose life I am comparing to my own. Then these feelings disappear and are quickly replaced by joy! It's wonderful!

Pause and Reflect

I have learnt that comparing myself to others never brings about good things in my life. If I compare myself favourably with someone else I feel superior. If it's an unfavourable comparison then I feel inferior. Neither is a Godly, Christ-like characteristic! Comparison is birthed in a place of insecurity. When you've been in an abusive relationship or situation, it's more likely that you become riddled with self-doubt and experience a deep-seated distrust in your own sense of worth and value. Even when people compliment you on a job well done, a new hair style or something you've created, you may find yourself internally doubting their sincerity or questioning their motives. At the bottom of it all, you just don't quite feel good enough – or as good as someone else.

There is a solution. One that will melt away the mistrust, self-doubt, unworthiness, sense of uselessness and replace it with a deep knowledge that you have a uniquely created place in this world. Recently, in a time of corporate worship, I sensed that Father God had swept me up into heaven and I was standing in the middle of an all-enveloping light which was emanating from Jesus. The light was warm and soft. It was an orange-gold-yellow sort of colour and I could feel it on my body. It was cone shaped and reminded me of an enormous spotlight. I was right in the middle of it. Totally covered. Within seconds I experienced a sensation of being loved in the most overwhelming way. I knew that I was loved – in a passionate, head-over-heels sort of way. Father God was expressing absolute delight over me. And I was loving it! Literally basking in it. No longer did I feel hidden – I was in the middle of Father God's spotlight! Being loved without measure. Knowing he wanted to be there right with me – loving me!

So, if you find yourself comparing yourself to others, favourably or unfavourably, make time to spend a few moments with our loving Father God. Quieten your heart, body and mind. Make yourself comfortable. Put on some worship music and sing along, giving him praise. Worship him. Then just ask him to show you how much he loves you. He's a very good Father and he will show you!

CHAPTER TEN

Unrestrained – Take Hold of Freedom

I stared at the book in my hands, *Freeing your Mind from Memories that Bind* by Fred and Florence Littauer. I had just been handed it by the Dean of Students in the Bible School we had attended. He had offered to take me through the counselling related to the book once I had read it if that was something I thought would help me. Knowing I had numerous memories of the hurt and trauma I had endured over the last more than eleven years, I thought this little book could be very helpful.

It had been barely a week since I had moved out of the family home with the children and into my own furnished place. Exhausted both physically and emotionally, I was sleeping as much as I could once the children were all in bed. Being organised enough to manage four children, school runs, meal times and a full time job gave me a focus and kept my mind occupied. Busyness was becoming my refuge while I was awake and exhaustion meant I didn't lie awake thinking either. Working in a Christian company meant I had support from kind and caring work colleagues, many of whom were friends too.

Reading this book provided me with a space in each day to allow my mind to come to rest and consider what I had been through in the light of what I was reading. Being analytical, I dissected pieces of my trauma and compared it with the stories in the book, putting little bits back together here and there, trying to make sense of the jigsaw puzzle of my adult life. Once in a while a piece seemed to make sense but not often. Realising it would be helpful to talk this through with someone, I decided to take up the offer of counselling.

Having agreed a weekly time slot with my boss, I found myself sitting in a comfortable armchair opposite the Dean. Having no idea what would or could happen, I was feeling a bit apprehensive. Was it madness to put myself through the pain of digging up and examining abusive experiences so soon after placing myself outside of harm's way? Would I be able to cope with it on an emotional level? Should I wait until I felt more whole, less ravaged? His first question confused me, "Why did a strong, confident person like you stay in a relationship like that for so long? Others would have left when it started." I didn't have an answer. I didn't know why I put up with it. I knew I wanted my marriage to work and I had prayed a lot about it. But I didn't know why I had not taken myself out of a situation where I was being hurt, misused and abused. The Dean asked more questions. What value did I place on myself? What did I think my rights were as a woman? As a wife? A mother? I struggled to formulate answers. I knew how I didn't want to be treated but I wasn't sure how I should be treated. We ended that first session with a statement, "The answer to why you stayed so long may lie in your childhood."

A few evenings later, once the children were in bed, I stood in the kitchen making myself a cup of coffee waiting for the water to boil and then stirring the milk into it. Staring out of the window into the distance, I suddenly came to a realisation: my mother had not liked me as a child or so it seemed to me. This heartfelt thought took my breath away. Tears started to roll down my cheeks as I remembered things I had shut away for a long time.

I was the eldest of six children and was born when my mother was just sixteen and three quarters. She and my dad (who was eighteen and a half) had married when she was four months pregnant. By age nineteen, she had three young daughters and by age twenty-two we had emigrated overseas, where she went on to bear three more children without the support of an extended family. Finding it difficult to cope, my mother became emotionally volatile and obsessive about housecleaning. As the eldest, I did all I could to protect my younger siblings from her angry outbursts and to keep the house immaculate. Amidst the turmoil and emotional instability, I tried hard to bring some sense of stability and calm at home. Taking responsibilities meant for an adult led to migraines at a very young age. Staring at my coffee, I realised all my efforts had not made my mother love me more but rather these efforts had probably made her feel inadequate and therefore she'd grown to dislike me. To her, it must have looked like I could do what she couldn't – I was calm and able to manage my emotions or so it seemed.

In my bedroom I sat and cried wholeheartedly. I expressed my hurt and disappointment at not feeling liked and loved by my mother as I grew up. I took time to make sure I understood and felt what that meant to me as a child. I had run away from home on a few occasions and remembered her helping to pack a bag for me as I did so rather than persuading me to stay. This lack of feeling liked and loved and denying my own emotions to keep a semblance of peace at home, had formed the foundation for me accepting and living through an emotionally volatile marriage, accepting it as normal. Had I experienced a secure loving relationship as a child feeling nurtured and protected and allowed to experience childhood emotions safely, I probably would not have stayed in that marriage relationship. Then I forgave my mother. Let her go. I gave her to Father God and allowed his comfort and nurture to envelop me and heal my pain.

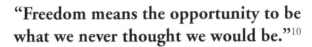

"Freedom means the opportunity to be what we never thought we would be."[10]

Daniel J Boorstin

My very first memory is of me trying to quieten down my crying baby sister because I didn't want her to upset my mother. I was two years old and my mother was just about nineteen and pregnant with her third child. Even at such a young age I felt a sense of responsibility to keep the peace at home.

As previously mentioned, we moved overseas as a family when I was nearly six in search of a better life and certain work. I admire my parents for taking this courageous decision. It cannot have been easy to move away from the support and security of a large family. We arrived with just ten shillings in my Dad's pocket and our first few weeks were spent in a large block of flats. I knew money was scarce and also that my dad smoked, so I set about picking up all the cigarette butts in the grounds of the flats, removing their paper and saving the tobacco into a plastic carrier bag. My heart was to make sure my Dad didn't go without and, even as a young child,

---

10. The Daniel J. Boorstin Reader (Modern Library), Daniel J. Boorstin, 1995, Modern Library Edition.

I thought I could do something about that. However, the old, used tobacco went into the bin and I was reprimanded.

I often looked after my younger two sisters and when my brother was born and I was eight years old, my mother had postnatal depression so I would get up with him in the night too. I really didn't mind. I wanted to be useful and feel appreciated. This need for a sense of value and worth led to me doing all sorts of household chores and gardening as well as helping to manage my younger siblings' more childlike behaviour. I was a good girl and did as I was told, very rarely straying outside of the lines I was given.

By the age of seven I was experiencing migraine headaches. Over the years, I have discovered that my body doesn't like dairy products and tolerates only small amounts of milk chocolate and no dark chocolate at all. But, as a child, even when I didn't eat these foods, I'd still get migraines accompanied by vomiting which meant I couldn't keep painkillers down either. I think these headaches surfaced as I took responsibility for adult roles at a much too early age.

I took these feelings of responsibility into my marriage. During the first four years I tried to assert myself and my values but heated discussions and physical, emotional and sexual abuse would ensue. After those first four years I stopped trying to change things. I decided I needed to manage the situation differently and so when things weren't going well, I took responsibility for this and blamed myself. What could I do differently? How could I make sure all was well in my home? I had the children's well-being to look out for.

Of course, I wasn't perfect and I had attitudes that needed changing too but I went too far: I took responsibility for things that should never have been mine. When you decide to stay in an abusive relationship, it's my opinion that you will probably inevitably take on responsibility for behaviours that are not your fault. I did. This is especially true when you are being told that something you did or said caused it anyway. Or even just being yourself caused it. It's hard not to feel responsible then.

In my case I was having Bible verses hurled at me too. I wasn't submissive enough. I didn't honour my husband. I wasn't teachable. I shouldn't be wearing make-up. I was proud and much more. My relationship with God was good and I knew he loved me. But these sorts of words would creep into my everyday thoughts and distort my view of myself. I'd feel responsible for his mood swings – if I was kinder, a better wife, could cook better, maybe he would be different too. He's not like this with others, it must be me. I'll change, I'll make this different. It's my responsibility.

I lived like this for many years – feeling a burden of responsibility for making my marriage better. I should have talked about it to someone but I didn't – I was ashamed. It would be an admission of failure. If I tried hard enough, I could make this work. If I prayed more and believed more, he would change. This was my responsibility. I kept going until I came to the end of what I could do. When I realised nothing was helping anymore, things were getting worse not better, my children were at risk and his thought processes were becoming more bizarre, I decided to leave. My sense of responsibility had taken me so far but couldn't take me and my children into safety.

A few years later I engaged in a few more counselling sessions with a wonderfully kind and wise lady. My then fiancé (now husband) and I had sat through the first of six group marriage preparation classes and I had come undone. We had been looking at what it meant to be "one" in the context of marriage. I realised instantly that I never wanted to be one with anyone ever again – I had nearly lost myself trying to do that! Speaking to our Pastor afterwards, he arranged these counselling sessions. One of the things she picked up on straight away was that I carried an inappropriate sense of responsibility for just about anything – so we unpicked this. Sought Father God's wisdom, prayed and I gained more freedom. This is an area I continue to lay before our Father God. It's an ongoing part of my journey into increasing levels of freedom!

Pause and Reflect

Romans 12:2 (Passion Translation) says, "Stop imitating the ideals and opinions of the culture around you, but be inwardly transformed by the Holy Spirit through *a total reformation of how you think.* This will empower you to discern God's will as you live a beautiful life, satisfying and perfect in his eyes" (italics added).

I don't think it's possible to gain true freedom without committing to reforming how you think about yourself, others, the world around you and God. Especially if you have endured abuse. Any traumatic life event can distort the way we view life and how we think. We develop patterns of thought that affect the way we live our lives. All of our behaviours, our ways of living, have their birth place in our thoughts. Even our emotions start with our thoughts. The good news is that we can change our feelings, our behaviours and ultimately our lives when we change the way we think. This verse explains that. When we have a "total transformation of how we think" there is a strong connection with the power of the Holy Spirit inwardly transforming us. We are empowered to discern God's will and live a beautiful and satisfying life! How wonderful is that!

God's word is amazing. It has the power to wash away our old ways of thinking. Ephesians 5:25b–26 (The Passion Translation) says, "For he (Christ Jesus) died for us, sacrificing himself to make us holy and pure, cleansing us through the showering of the pure water of the Word of God."

If you want to change the way you think about yourself, others or a situation, you need to find out what the Bible has to say about it. This is easier than you think it may be – there are websites to help you with this! My favourite one is biblegateway.com. You can type in a word and then it comes up with a list of bible verses for that word. So let's have a practice for how this could work:

1. Ask Father God to show you something that you have thoughts about that are not based in truth. Something that needs to be showered with the pure water of the word of God. I grew up in a home where money was very scarce. As an example, let's use the thought that I will always struggle financially. In other words that I am poor and may have just enough but never have more than enough.

2. If this is the wrong way of thinking, how do we determine what would be the right way of thinking? It's often the opposite. In this example the right way of thinking would be that because I am a child of the creator of the universe, I am rich and can have all my needs met. In fact, Father God delights in blessing me.

3. To help me change my way of thinking about this, I want to find out what the Bible says about it. When I put the word "rich" into the search tool on biblegateway.com (searching the New Testament only, otherwise I could end up with loads of verses to read through), I find this

verse in Philippians 4:19, "And my God will meet all your needs according to the riches of his glory in Christ Jesus." This is the verse I will memorise and write out. It will go on my fridge and in my purse until I have washed away my old way of thinking and have come more fully to realise that the Jesus I follow is rich beyond my imagination and can provide for all my needs at any time! He is the source of my supply. I will always have enough or even more than enough.

4. There are also lots of other Bible verses that have something to say about riches. Some speak about the riches of God's grace and some warn against putting our hope in worldly riches rather than in Father God. Others tell the story of a young leader who would do anything Jesus asked him to except give up his riches. These are also good sections of the Bible to read and understand. They will help us gain a greater understanding of God's overall view of riches.

5. It takes a little bit of time to find the Bible verses that help us to bring about a different way of thinking – but it's worth it. Hebrews 4:12 tells us, "For the word of God is alive and active. Sharper than any double edged sword, it penetrates even to dividing soul and spirit, joints and marrow; it judges the thoughts and attitudes of the heart." God's word is a powerful part of our armoury in our journey to gain ever more freedom and become more like Jesus!

6. Go ahead – try this out for a different topic that is relevant to you.

CHAPTER ELEVEN

Unrestrained – Become Powerful

I was screaming loudly but couldn't work out why. There was pressure on my mouth. A couple of short hours ago I had fallen asleep in my bed. I could hear a muffled voice to my right, "Stop screaming, stop!" A man's voice. One I recognised. My screams subsided and my eyes shot open. He was dressed in black with a balaclava over his face. Realising I had stopped screaming, he released his hand from my mouth and pulled the balaclava off his head. It was him! Somehow he had managed to get into my house and right into my bedroom! I moved quickly, scrambling to the other side of the bed, landing with my feet on the floor. "Why are you here? How did you get in?"

He had moved quickly too and grabbed my arm, forcing me into a sitting position on the bed. Keeping hold of me, he started explaining. He had been to church that evening and the pastor had been preaching on the theme of God having a blueprint for each of our lives. He told me he had his hunting knife in the sitting room next door and he was going to tie me up and then I could decide which one of the children I wanted to see die first. He was going to kill them one at a time. It would all be my fault as I had left him and that wasn't right. He would leave me alive so I could give birth to four more children who could take on the blueprints God had prepared for the ones I had caused to die.

I struggled, trying to free myself from his grasp but not wanting to make too much noise. I didn't want the children to wake up. That would aggravate the situation. I needed to keep them out of this and as safe as possible. My struggling only made things worse. He grabbed me with both hands pushing me into the bed then climbing on top of me. He then held me in position with one hand while he pulled a sock out of a pocket and thrust it into my mouth. Realising he had come prepared, fear rose within me. Next, he grabbed the telephone cable next to my bed, yanking it out of the wall. Using this, he tied my hands behind my back. I couldn't speak but I was making sounds, pleading with him to stop. He continued to sit on top of me, taunting me, blaming me. Suddenly, he stopped. He stood up and moved to the ensuite bathroom. I could hear him drinking water.

As quickly and quietly as I could, I stood up on the bed. Moving every possible part of my mouth I tried desperately to push the sock out of it, all the while twisting and turning my hands, pulling them little by little out of the restrictive telephone cord. Just as he re-entered the bedroom, both the sock and the cord fell to the bed. Immediately, I started talking as fast and persuasively as I could. So much was at stake. I had made a mistake. I would come back to him. We could sort it out. Of course he was upset. Who wouldn't be in his situation? He was right. It was all my fault. We could make it better. We would come back. We would start all over again. A new beginning. I lied and lied. My life, my children's lives, depended up on it.

Before my eyes he started to relax. I could see he was starting to believe me. I carried on talking, quietly, quickly. He wanted to wake the children up and tell them we were all going to live together again. I resisted. It was late and they would be tired and grumpy. It was best to wait until the next morning. However, he wasn't ready to leave. This could escalate again. I suggested he lie down and sleep until they woke up. He agreed but only if I took off my pyjamas and slept next to him. Everything in me revolted but what might the alternative be? I acquiesced.

Once he had accepted the next lie I told him, the one where having sex would be better if it signified the new beginning back in our own home rather than now, he slept. Albeit rather fitfully. In contrast, lying very still next to him, I couldn't sleep at all. Thoughts, ideas, pictures whirled round in my mind. Could I make it to the kitchen, pick out the best knife, creep back into the bedroom and thrust it into his heart without waking him up? Imagining the sensation of pushing a knife into flesh made me realise I couldn't do it. I was still scared. Terrified, in fact: but after all was said and done, right now, he was asleep and not terrorising me. No, I couldn't do it.

Unexpectedly, he started speaking, interrupting my thoughts. It wasn't going to work. He had done some terrible things. Things I didn't know about. I reassured him. It would be alright. He was becoming agitated. He wanted to tell me: he had spent time with prostitutes. It would be alright, I said. I could forgive that. There was more: he had had sex with animals when he was younger. Then, the deepest revelation, I suspected: he had been abused by his oldest brother when he was a child. Under other circumstances I would have delved deeper, listened carefully, but right now I was focused on surviving. I kept talking using reassuring words and language, lulling him back into sleep.

This unexpected and unsolicited vulnerability may have made him more suggestable when I woke him up as the sun rose, explaining that the children would be confused to find him here. It would be best for him to sneak out and give me time to explain to them that we were moving back. He left quietly through the patio doors he had lifted from their hinges when entering earlier on while I was asleep. As soon as I heard him drive away, I called the police and then my small group leader. Having held it all together up to this point, I could no longer keep the tears and shaking in check.

Having taken a statement and organised private time to talk to a female officer, the police wanted to arrest him immediately. My eldest son was soon to leave on a week long school trip and I knew he would be expecting his father to see him off as he left on the bus, so I convinced them it was in my child's best interest to wait to arrest him until after my son was safely on his way. As it was, the police couldn't find him afterwards and so it wasn't until the end of the day that he was taken into custody. For now, I was safe.

"Powerlessness is an excruciating pain; it is torture insurmountable."[11]

Richelle E. Goodrich

Lack of control over personal actions and decisions is usually a defining characteristic of the life of a person in an abusive relationship. No one makes a conscious choice to be abused and misused. In fact, the sense of loss of control over your life

11. Making Wishes: Quotes, Thoughts, & a Little Poetry for Every Day of the Year, Richelle E. Goodrich, 2015, CreateSpace Independent Publishing Platform.

can often lead to deep seated feelings of powerlessness, despair and depression. In my own life, while I was being sexually abused, and knew that in that moment I could do nothing to stop or change that abuse, I would "separate" myself from my body: I would imagine myself floating around the room looking down at myself. This helped me to cope with the situation as I could distance myself from the physical and emotional pain I was feeling. I seemed to be outside of that – just a shell of a body experiencing what was happening in the moment. For me, this didn't mean I never fully experienced the pain, just rather that I delayed the full intensity of it for a later time when I was on my own. It helped me cope with the immediate sense of powerlessness by giving me a tiny piece of control back in the moment.

I hated feeling powerless and I know that I am not the only one. One person I spoke to about their abuse despises themselves for being helpless, to the extent that they intensely dislike having any attention given to helping them deal with the ongoing effects of the abuse in their now adult life. Acknowledging their need for the help of others seems to accentuate the feelings of powerlessness they had then and continue to have to this day.

When there are areas of your life which are beyond your control, it becomes an almost natural response to take control of all other areas. This can be detrimental too. Sometimes this is evidenced in obsessive behaviours such as excessive cleaning, handwashing, security, eating, purging and so much more. Each of us is unique and we all react differently. Personally, I like a tidy house and I have had to train myself over the years that it's OK to leave a used coffee cup on the coffee table until the next morning. A sink full of dirty dishes or a laundry basket half full of washing waiting to be ironed is a wonderful picture of victory in my life.

I have a natural strength for looking ahead into the future and considering what that may look like. When I was living through the years of an abusive marriage, this strength took on a different function: I used it to manage and control everything I could to try to make sure nothing took me by surprise. If I knew what was coming up, I'd be able to control the effects of it and so lessen the likelihood of anything unsettling him and then me bearing the brunt of this. This was not a very effective strategy and it often didn't work. It did mean though that I didn't feel quite so powerless and devoid of hope. I was being proactive. I was taking back some control.

I like walking and when I'm with someone (or in a group) I like to know where we're going in some detail before we set off. I find myself getting annoyed and unhappy if I feel information is being kept from me. I'm surprised that not everyone is as insistent as I am in knowing the details. To this day, I like to feel in control and fully empowered. This may be true of many people, those who have survived abuse and those who have never been abused. The fact that I lose my peace if I am not in possession of all the facts and can get really annoyed and even angry is a sure sign I am still on a journey in this area of my life. I am still learning and healing.

One thing I do know: I have a loving heavenly Father who knows me, delights in me and leads me into green pastures and beside still waters. As I spend time in his presence my heart is at peace and full of contentment. I can lay all my anxieties and stress at his feet and he will melt them away, replacing them with his complete sense of well-being. When we moved back to the UK, it was with a written agreement that my eldest four children would be sent overseas to spend time with their father twice a year at our expense. The first time I had to put my children on an aeroplane to travel overseas for four weeks, I sobbed. To my mind there was a very real possibility that I would never get them back. As I wasn't with them, I wouldn't know on a day by day basis if they were safe and being looked after properly. Everything about this situation made me feel extremely powerless and anxious. There was only one thing I could do – bring it all to my Father God. Through the tears I prayed, telling Father God all I felt, detailing my every fear. When I had spent myself and had no more to say and no tears left to cry, the Holy Spirit came and rested on me and in me giving me the peace my heart craved. I knew then I had to give up the control of my children's circumstances into the hands of a loving Father God and let him walk their journeys with them. It was a place of rest and submission. I faced the idea that they may not come back but that God would still be with them. The burden I had carried so long of being their only protector lifted. My powerful Father God would always do a far better job than I could.

I am in the process of learning that there isn't any freedom in hanging onto control. Freedom comes when we give ourselves into the hands of God, fully submitted, enjoying the grace and strength that he gives us, facing each moment with our heads on his shoulder.

Pause and Reflect

We were created to live powerful lives. God's plan right from the beginning was for us to rule and reign over the earth (Genesis 1:28). Our God given default mode is to live our lives feeling safe, secure, loved, fulfilled, making wise decisions, feeling powerful and content.

The Kingdom of God that we live in is an upside down kingdom. We are servant leaders. The humble receive grace and promotion. The way up is down. God's power works through love, not position or status. We are made in his image and created to be powerful people.

- We are children of the Creator of the universe.
- Our Father God delights in doing the impossible in us and through us.
- He has created each of us to be unique and uniquely gifted.
- Each of us has a significant role to play in furthering the kingdom of God here on earth that only we can do.
- Every one of us has a voice and something to say in both words and actions.
- Our Father God delights in partnering with us!

Are you, like me, trying to live a powerful life through exercising control in different ways and situations? I'm learning that letting go of control is liberating! It frees up time to focus on loving people and God more deeply. God's wonderful power shows up all the time when we love him, others and ourselves well.

Take a moment – what is there in your own life that you are keeping control over that you could let go of? Be powerful – let go!

CHAPTER TWELVE

Unrestrained – Thwart Defensiveness

Sitting on a solid, uncomfortable wooden bench in the corridor outside a door leading to the courtroom for my case, I waited silently for the lawyer who had been assigned to me. A friend from my church small group had come with me to lend emotional support. We had prayed together during the car journey here and she had felt that God would "make your righteous reward shine like the dawn, your vindication like the noonday sun" (Psalm 37:6). I had never been in court before and so I was feeling quite apprehensive. It hadn't helped that only a few moments ago I had seen my husband arrive with his lawyers who, on spotting me, had deftly led him off into a side room. I had heard that he had hired two lawyers and was sure to be found not guilty and allowed to go home. I was very nervous about what that would mean for me.

He had not been allowed bail and therefore had been kept in jail for just over a month while waiting for this case to be heard. The counsellor had been asked to testify at his bail hearing and he had told the court that my life would be in danger if my husband was allowed to await his trial outside of a jail cell. His family were furious. He was the middle child of seven siblings. They were a close-knit family who saw each other very regularly and knew everything about the goings on in each part of this extended family. About every six months there would be a minor or major explosion and one part of the family would fall out with the rest of them. Thankfully, as an outsider, I didn't often get drawn into these adult squabbles. However, this time I was seen as the manipulative instigator of the hardship their son and brother was being forced to endure. Their anger was very overtly directed at me. He had been placed in a multi-racial jail and they had to queue with people of all races when waiting to see him. Politically, they were quite right wing and thus they saw this as an insult brought about by my actions. His mother and father were getting on in years and their children considered it a disgrace that I was responsible for them having to stand (sometimes for long periods of time) in the hot sun in close proximity to people from social classes beneath theirs. This was not what they were used to or had come to expect in the course of their lives. In their eyes, I was the originator of their inconvenience and suffering.

After only a brief discussion with my lawyer I was led into the courtroom which was presided over by one male magistrate. Once the formalities were over I was asked to take the stand. Having taken an oath to tell the truth, I lifted my head and eyes and realised I was going to give my testimony with my husband, flanked by his lawyers, directly in front of me. Directing my gaze above their heads, I was startled to see that a large number of my husband's family were standing in the elevated public gallery just slightly to the left of him. I immediately asked the magistrate if they could wait outside as I found their presence intimidating but he refused, saying they had a right to be there – it was a public gallery after all. I would have to manage my feelings of anxiety and stress.

As I answered the questions my lawyer asked me, I kept my eyes on just him and spoke as clearly and truthfully as I could, describing the events of that break-in night in as much detail as I could remember. Interrupting me almost every sentence, the magistrate kept asking me to slow down as he was trying to take notes. Feeling hemmed in on every side – by a seemingly unsympathetic magistrate, a posse of in-laws and a team of three smug, smiling defendants – I was struggling to keep my thoughts together. At one point I glanced up only to catch the eye of a sister-in-law obviously praying in tongues. That picture so shocked me that I completely lost my train of thought and stopped speaking. How could that be? How could she be using a spiritual gift given by God as a weapon against me, also child of God? It didn't make sense. I asked the magistrate to repeat what I had just said so I could retrace my thoughts and carry on where I had left off but he refused to. Taking a moment to breathe as slowly as I could, I then resumed speaking, my confidence shaken. His lawyers then began their interrogation. Did I think my husband was perhaps obsessed with me? Why had I written him encouraging notes while we were married? I couldn't work out why I was being asked things about the years we were married and nothing about the night of the break-in and attack on me. Nothing was making sense.

After only a relatively short time of waiting, we were called back into the courtroom. The charge against him was Grievous Bodily Harm but he was found guilty of only Common Assault and, as he had already served just over a month in jail, he was immediately released. Instruction was given that I was to allow the children to see him as he had not seen them while in jail. As it was already late in the afternoon, he would be collecting the children the next day. This didn't feel like justice!

Returning to work for a couple of hours, I met with my boss and explained what had happened. I was devastated that I had to trust my children into his care the next day. I didn't know if I could do this – anguish threatened to overwhelm me, tears came. My boss reassured me that God had each of them in his hands. He cared for them more than I did. Their father wouldn't dare take them away or hurt them or me now. He had a police record and he would be found and charged very quickly for anything to do with me or the children. I needed to hear all of this. Even more than this, I needed to get home into the presence of Father God where I could find comfort and strength again.

"The problem in defence is how far you can go without destroying from within what you are trying to defend from without."[12]

Dwight D. Eisenhower

Over the years I have often found myself fighting my own corner. Sometimes this has been over bigger issues but often it has been over small things – perhaps even unnecessary things. Being defensive about anything and everything just seemed to be part of me. I remember once being in a prayer counselling session where we were hearing the voice of God together about various aspects of my life. It was a wonderful time and God spoke very clearly to me though pictures, words and deep impressions. I came away feeling so blessed. One of the pictures God gave the counsellor was of two trees. Both were fully grown trees but one had deep roots and a full rounded

---

12. Revisiting the Concept of Defence in the Jus ad Bellum: The Dual Face of Defence Johanna Friman, 2017, Hart Publishing.

top of large branches and many leaves and much fruit. The other had shallower roots and therefore also fewer branches, leaves and fruit. Through this picture God was telling me that my roots had not been fully formed. Because of this, I felt like I always had to justify my place in the world. I had to make myself heard. Sometimes I was over assertive as a result – a bit pushy. I could be abrasive and had a bit of a hard edge.

I have had quite a lot to do with people who have been abused as children or adults (or both) over the years and I have noticed that this can be the case for many of them too. Many have an edge. People have told them they are pushy or even aggressive. This does not come from a desire to do others harm but often from a sense of needing to justify ourselves – convince others of our right to be. Our right to hold opinions. Our right to do. When, at some time in our lives, we have had the right to be heard, appreciated or valued taken from us, we subconsciously assert that right and do what we can to be seen and heard and valued. This often happens for many years after the abuse has stopped – it can be ongoing.

For me, seeing the picture of the two trees was just the very beginning of addressing this particular issue. I had been through lots of traditional counselling and this hadn't come up. However, I knew God was in it and so I started reflecting on this. I knew I wanted to fulfil my potential in Christ – to do all he had called me to do while on earth. If I went through the rest of my life feeling like I needed to prove my worth and/or justify my reason for being, while still loving God, I would be the lesser tree – bearing some fruit, providing some shade, making room for some birds and their nests. To become the fuller tree, I needed a miracle – a reset, a change of personal perspective, a paradigm shift. I needed to know who I really was and not just who I thought I was, or believed I was, in light of the responses of others to me.

I had already read the "in him" scriptures but I started doing so again (see appendix). I love the word of God and I am a firm believer in the power of the word of God to bring life to our very beings. I also know that we nearly always need to hear scriptures many times before they sink into our hearts and minds. So I started writing down the verses which spoke of who I am in Christ Jesus and reading them every day. I knew that by doing this, I was helping to rewire my thinking. This really did help. I became more confident in who I was because I am in Christ.

This is an ongoing journey of finding out who I am in God's eyes and what he has called me to be. I suspect that is the case for all of us! Moments of real breakthrough happen, I have found, as we pursue our Father God and his presence. Personally, it is the increasing revelation of being a daughter of my Father God that has brought me the most freedom to be who I am. That sense of knowing Father God's love as it settles on and in you when you are in his presence just seems to melt away all striving. I love worshipping him with other believers in a church or corporate setting. Father God comes and meets with us individually in such a powerful way so often when we put everything else aside and focus all our attention on him together. We are free just to be ourselves knowing he loves every bit of us. The more we do this together, the easier it becomes to practise this on our own as well. I am reminded of a monk called Brother Lawrence (Practising the Presence of God) whose main job was to cook and clean in the kitchen. He would peel potatoes or wash pots, then fall to the floor and wait on God, face down – and God would come! For me, even as I type up these words, I can feel the presence of Father God and sense the light touch of Jesus on my shoulders! How amazing is that! He loves us – as we are! I am his daughter and he delights in me. You are his child and he delights in you!

Knowing you are loved just as you are as a son or daughter of a loving Father God is such an important key to finding freedom and living a life content in who you are – loved, accepted, valued, worthy, significant, unique, gifted, a blessing, beautiful, adored, delightful, cared for and so much more! There is no-one like our Father God and there is no-one like you. He made you uniquely you and he loves you as you are. I encourage you to pursue his presence and rest in it. Be filled with a deep sense of your enduring identity as a child of Father God.

Pause and Reflect

A few years ago, I came across teaching on what it meant to have an "orphan heart". I continue to grow in my understanding of what this is and often realise that I am engaging in some "orphan thinking". In developing my understanding of what an "orphan heart" is it helped me to visualise the plight of a physical orphan. I have been to India and visited the slum areas there. It was heart breaking – the levels of poverty are shocking. However, the lives street children have on the streets are even worse. Those in the slums usually have parents looking out for them – those on the streets do not. They have to fend for themselves. Some are very young. Four or five years old. Physically, they are dirty, thin, barefooted, desperately hungry and clothed in rags. Psychologically, they often have a determination and focus that you wouldn't expect to see. Those who have been living on the streets for a while don't seem to be in a state of shock any longer. They've learnt how to survive. They know how to defend themselves and, in the main, keep themselves safe. Imagine – as dusk falls, as an orphan on the streets you pull out your woven mat and find a spot to lie down, seeking a little shelter beside large dustbins or inside a doorway. As you close your eyes, you know that if anyone tries to hurt you while you are in this vulnerable state called sleep, no-one will come to help you – you can only rely on yourself.

Although not physically orphans, those of us who have been through abuse often feel like that. We can only rely on ourselves. No-one is looking out for us. If they are, it's because they have to – it's their duty. Like the paid workers in a children's care home, they are doing a job. If we don't stand up for ourselves there is no-one else who will. We have to fight for our place in this world. Proving our worth is second nature. Even when someone is nice to us or recognises a gift or talent we have, we may nod and smile but inwardly we are thinking all sorts of self-preservation lies like, "They have to say that, they're Christians," or "I wonder what they say when I'm not here? I bet they talk about all the things I still need to work on then!" This is "orphan thinking" and we need to recognise it as such.

We are no longer orphans – we are blood bought children of Father God. Not only are we forgiven and brought into a wonderful relationship with him but we are also treasured, loved and liked!

- We have been given so many incredible gifts – everything we need to live a God-like life. 2 Peter 1:3 says, "His divine power has *given us everything we need for a godly life* through our knowledge of him who called us by his own glory and goodness" (italics added).

- We do have someone who will fight our cause for us – we are not alone. Jesus is actively praying for our success at any given moment. Romans 8:34, "Who then is the one who condemns? No one. Christ Jesus who died—more than that, who was raised to life – is at the right hand of God and is also interceding for us." The Passion Translation says he is praying for our "triumph" and the King James version says he "ever lives to make intercession for us". We are never on our own, not for a single minute – the prayers of Jesus cover us.

- We don't have to fight our battles on our own. Our Father God is waiting for us to confidently ask him for his help: Hebrews 4:16, "Let us then approach God's throne of grace with confidence, so that we may *receive mercy and find grace to help us in our time of need*" (italics added).

- We have the Holy Spirit who is given to us. Jesus told us in John 14:16-18, "And I will ask the Father, and he will give you another advocate to help you and be with you forever – the Spirit of truth. The world cannot accept him, because it neither sees him nor knows him. But you know him, for he lives with you and will be in you. *I will not leave you as orphans; I will come to you*" (italics added). He is our advocate – he speaks up on our behalf. Whereas once we may have felt like we were not heard, we now have another who advocates on our behalf!

- This same Holy Spirit prays for us! Romans 8:26, "In the same way, the Spirit *helps us in our weakness*. We do not know what we ought to pray for, but the *Spirit himself intercedes* for us through wordless groans" (italics added). He helps us when we are feeling weak and prays for us. We are not alone! We can depend on him. We no longer have to be self-reliant and fight our own corner.

We have Father, Son and Holy Spirit interceding for us and coming to our aid when we are weak. The next time you find yourself, like me, jumping to your own defence as a knee jerk reaction, take a few seconds. Remind yourself that heaven is in your corner and thwart your own defensiveness.

CHAPTER THIRTEEN

Unrestrained – Speak Life Giving Words

"What's a whore, Mummy?" asked one of the girls as she bounced through the door after a day out with her father. This question was very quickly followed by my eldest son trying to quieten her. "But Daddy says Mummy's a whore and I want to know what it is!" she insisted. I was relieved – I had the children back home with me safe and sound and it seemed as if they had had a good time with their father. They had spent the day with his extended family, swimming and playing. He hadn't run away with them, he hadn't kept them overnight, they were here back with me, under my roof. It was time for baths and bed. Tomorrow was another day and it would bring its own challenges.

Each time they arrived home after a day with their father, I would need to spend some time answering awkward questions in an attempt to protect their young minds from concepts that should have been beyond their years. But they did always come back to me.

Eventually, I moved with the children – and his hard won permission – back to the UK on the proviso that I would send them to see him (at our expense) twice a year. They would often spend four or five weeks with him and his family over the British summer school holidays. It would take us just about the same number of weeks to settle them back into sensible routines and unpack some of the ideas and values that they had picked up while away. We didn't want the children to internalise racist or sexist ideas and values. We had to use wisdom and chose often to avoid head on confrontations and arguments. Instead, when we could, we waited for quieter moments when we were enjoying being together, to expose lies and instil truth.

On one occasion, in the normal course of a working day, I answered a telephone call to find I was speaking to him – being asked to pick him up from our local train station. He had come to the UK to surprise the children. They were delighted while I was shocked, physically trembling and feeling nauseous. I felt I was being forced not only to see him face to face, but to help him get around a town, county and country unfamiliar to him. I would have to come into close proximity to him, alone together in my car. With notice, I could have arranged something else and prepared the children. I felt vulnerable and bewildered.

To make matters even more chaotic, the children begged me to have him live with us in our house, to have him eat with us, socialise with us. He walked self-assuredly into my kitchen, putting meat products in the fridge, assuming he had the right to do so. I had been caught off guard and couldn't work out how to respond. I seemed to have slipped back into a subservient role, doing as I was told.

I had remarried just over a year before but my husband was at work and had, so far, no idea of what had just happened. Eventually, I managed to get away into a separate room and call him. Although a gentle man, he was clear that the children's father could not stay with us in our house while he was in the country. I was to find him a bed and breakfast place and point him in the direction of local restaurants.

Once he arrived home from work and I had made sure the children's father was settled into a B&B, we talked to the children about why their father was staying where he was. In truth, they didn't really understand. The next few weeks were truly confusing for them, especially the boys as they were older. Their father talked of moving to the UK and living closer to them but then would change his mind and instead invite them to come and live with him overseas, any time they wanted to. Dread filled my heart at the thought of losing my boys. I doubted very much that he would make sure they went to school or take them to church. But, more than this, I feared the example he might set for them. For me, it was an excruciating few weeks. I felt like I was living on the edge of a cliff, about to fall off. I could barely eat and slept fitfully. I did the only thing I had left to me – I prayed. My husband and I prayed together – fervently, often with tears.

After a few weeks, he left as suddenly as he had arrived. He had come to the realisation that he didn't want to live in the UK. He needed to get back home and get on with his life. I was hugely relieved. He had, however, destabilised my eldest son, who was thirteen at the time, and it took many months for him to settle again.

Regularly, while the children were with him for their holiday weeks over the summer, he would call me. He took this opportunity to make sure that I realised what a terrible mother I was. I was told that the children were unhappy with me. I had never been, and would never be, a good homemaker. I didn't know how to make the children happy or anyone else who came into my home. I was a terrible cook, housekeeper, homemaker, wife and mother. No good to anyone. It was at those moments that I would be most concerned that he wouldn't send the children back to me. But they did come home – safely – while they were young.

My middle son, after numerous encouraging telephone calls from his father, insisted on going to live with him overseas. He was fifteen at the time and unhappy at school too. I did all I could to persuade him otherwise and wept when he left, my heart broken. One of the girls called me while on holiday with her siblings after she had completed her GCSEs. She had decided to stay with her father and do her matric there. She wasn't coming home. It was devastating news compounded by the harsh, derogatory criticisms levied at me over the phone by her father after she had told me her news. Her twin sister came home and started her A Levels but missed her sister so much, she decided to join her too. These were dark days for me.

In hindsight, years later, I can see the hand of God even in this. Their father died an early death. The children spent some years with him before he died and I believe this to be the grace of God at work in their lives. All of the children currently live in the UK and I see all of them regularly – God has been kind to me.

"If you wish to know the mind of a man, listen to his words."[13]

Chinese Proverb

Words are impregnated with a mysterious and powerful ability. Most people no longer believe that "words will never hurt me". The Bible tells us that life and death are in the power of the

---

13. Civilization's Quotations: Life's Ideal, edited by Richard Alan Krieger, 2007, Algora Publishing.

tongue – and anyone who has been on the receiving end of either positive encouragement or verbal abuse knows this to be true. You can come away from a verbal assessment of you as a person or your abilities elated or crushed.

It's commonly accepted now that the words themselves, in any form of communication, count for about only seven percent of the message received. A whopping fifty-five percent of the message received is through the body language of the person speaking and thirty-eight percent is conveyed through their tone of voice. Confusion reigns when these three areas don't line up, for example when someone is being told they are loved while being beaten up and yelled at.

Words become even more powerful when spoken by someone we trust or someone who we feel we should trust, such as a person in a position of authority. It's easier to dismiss a nasty comment from someone who has just met you than from someone you are living your life with. Equally, it's harder to accept the positive encouragement of a counsellor you have just started seeing when the trusted mother, father, husband, wife, brother or sister you have been living with has dismantled you with their words over many years. In the same way, the length of time they have known you may also affect how much importance you consciously, or even unconsciously, attach to their words. Sometimes, you don't even realise you place so much store in their words and opinion of you. That was the case for me. A counsellor pointed out to me that I was always referring back to what my husband had said about any given situation even after I had left him. His words still held sway over me. They had taken on a life of their own within my mind. Even when he himself was no longer speaking these words, they were entrenched enough to make themselves known again – they seemed to have enduring power.

The strength of emotion that underpins the words being spoken can seem to drive them into your mind and soul.

Shouting, sneering, ridiculing, snarling and so forth can feel intimidating and evoke all sorts of emotions in the hearer: fear, humiliation, shame, guilt, worthlessness and powerlessness. These emotions then serve as a further filter while the nastiness and manipulation continue – the words themselves swirl around in your being, forming an unhelpful fog that clouds your own sense of worth and value. The words themselves, together with the emotion and tone they are spoken with, become toxic and harmful to you.

If the body language (facial expressions, physical stance, hand, feet and leg movements) works together to underscore the derogatory comments being made, those words become a powerful weapon in the mouth of the person speaking them.

To add to this, when you are in an abusive relationship of any kind, the phrases spoken to you and about you are often repeated many times over. Instead of becoming oblivious to their effects, you may find yourself internalising them even though you try hard not to believe them. The words themselves are lies and always have been lies. In my case I was not a bad mother – I was a very good mother and continue to be so. I am very apt at creating a loving home environment, having done so in many houses we have lived in.

But words don't give up their power just because you have walked away from the abuse. I have found that it's important to recognise the lies you believe about yourself and do something about them quickly. Some of those lies will be the direct result of things spoken over you and to you. When I become aware of a lie I am believing, this is what I do:

1. I identify the lie.

2. In prayer, I repent of believing the lie and I break agreement with it.

3. I ask God what truth he wants to give me in exchange for the lie.

4. I thank him for this and ask the Holy Spirit to take it deep into my heart and mind.

5. I write it down and remind myself of it daily until I feel I have made it my own.

Let me give you an example. I recently became aware that I would often say I was not a nurturing, pastoral type of person. I had taken this lie on board a long time ago because my husband had accused me often of being hard, unfeeling, unkind and unloving because I didn't meet his needs. I recognised that those words still had some power over me but I knew them to be a lie and so why would I still say this about myself? Just today, someone told me I was a loving and kind person and that he had seen that evidenced in the way I led a group. I had smiled and shrugged that encouragement off. Later, I felt the holy Spirit nudge me – there was a lie I was believing.

The lie was that I was not nurturing and not pastoral. The lie was that I was unfeeling and hard.

In prayer, I came before our loving Father God and repented out loud of believing that lie. I broke agreement with that lie. I determined not to partner with it anymore. I would see myself as Father God saw me.

I then asked our loving Father God what truth he wanted to give me in exchange for this lie. He then showed me many hundreds of people standing with upturned radiant faces. These were people that had gained freedom and were gratefully looking upwards towards Father God, receiving his love for them. I had been part of their journey in gaining that freedom. My truth was that Father God had created me to love, nurture, pastor and bless people. My lie had been limiting me in my purpose here on earth in extending the Kingdom of God.

I then expressed my gratitude to Father God. He is so good and he is always wanting to give us good gifts and ever more freedom. I asked the Holy Spirit to take this new found truth deep into my heart and mind – to engraft it there.

Lastly, I wrote this truth in simple words on a piece of paper and put it in my notebook to read daily.

Proverbs 18:21 (Amplified version) says, "Death and life are in the power of the tongue, and those who love it and indulge it will eat its fruit and bear the consequences of their words." Words are indeed mysterious and powerful. God's words particularly so – let's speak his words over our own lives.

Pause and Reflect

The Bible tells us that Jesus has the words of eternal life (John 6:68). He speaks those wonderful life-giving words over us. We are part of his family and can come into his presence anytime we like – what a privilege and what joy! Our Father God is good and there is not the slightest hint of a shadow in him. James 1:17 (The Passion Translation) says, "Every gift God freely gives us is *good and perfect*, streaming down from the Father of lights, who shines from the heavens with no hidden shadow or darkness and is never subject to change" (italics added). Every word Father God sings out over us is good – there are no lies, no shadows in them.

The battle with lies comes from ourselves. So often, we have internalised the lies others have spoken about us and made them part of our own thought life and self-talk. The challenge is to catch ourselves doing this, name the lie and take it to God to find out what he thinks of it! Above is an example of how I dealt with one life limiting lie. It's important to recognise that the lies we tell ourselves don't only negatively affect our own lives but often limit the positive influence and effect we could be having on others.

Some of us may believe many, many lies about ourselves and it is possible to have them all miraculously washed away. But if that doesn't happen in one episode, take heart and identify just one lie and start with that. Be determined. Pick the lies off one at a time. Use the five step process I gave as an example above. Yes, you may still be telling yourself lots of unhelpful negative things but you will also be telling yourself one positive, life-giving truth too. Eventually, if you keep doing this, you'll be hearing and believing more life-giving truths than negative life sapping lies – and you will be changed! Words are powerful and can bring life and new freedoms!

CHAPTER FOURTEEN

Unrestrained – Expect Restoration

It would soon be midnight and I needed to change out of my glitzy circus costume and get into my wedding dress. Friends took the twins into an adjoining room to help them change into their fairy, flower girl dresses. The best man, my middle son, was with my husband-to- be already dressed in his matching ring master suit. My eldest, Dracula cape in place, was to walk me down the aisle as soon as I was dressed. Nerves were getting the better of me and I was shaking. A close friend pressed a glass of champagne into my hand.

It was a humid New Year's Eve (overseas) and friends and family were now waiting outside under the stars for me to walk down the candlelit pathway. We had chosen a circus theme and all, including our wonderful church minister, were dressed accordingly. Our talented worship team were entertaining the guests – some dancing, others sitting around tables eating. Many had been here since about nine o'clock. As we passed midnight, the wedding ceremony began. Scripture and words of wisdom filled the night time air. The groom sang, "You look wonderful tonight" by Erik Clapton, rings were exchanged and congratulations ensued – it was a wonderfully joyous, and slightly bizarre event. We loved it!

The journey to this point had not been without its challenges though. My wonderful new husband had been a bachelor all his adult life. Needless to say, commitment had not been his strong point. He had lived with indecision: what if someone better, more suited to him was just around the corner? How would he cope with not only a new wife and life partner but four children as well? There was a volatile ex-husband in the frame as well.

Once the ex-husband realised there was someone else in my life, he stalked him. One day, he confronted my new man while he was in a shopping mall – verbally threatening to "take him out" with a crossbow if he didn't leave me alone. On another occasion, the ex-husband seemed sullen and depressed, complaining to him that I had woken up one day and suddenly declared that I didn't love him anymore for no rhyme or reason. He warned him that this would be his fate too. Sometimes, he just followed him but at a distance, only just visible.

The children were drawn into this too. He made them promise that they would never call my new husband Dad. When they were with him, he questioned them intensely, wanting to know where and when they had been with the new man.

He vacillated between angry confrontation and desperate despair. He followed me too although I hadn't realised this at first. Sometimes, I would visit my husband-to-be at his flat which was in a building where every visitor had to sign in and out. He bribed the security staff, copied the sign in sheets and then accused me of neglecting the children with both Social Services and my church leaders. Both bodies called me for further information and then gave me assurances that no action would be taken. I was relieved but also anxious, realising my every move was being carefully monitored by him.

On the eve of my wedding, he called me to say that he would forgive me, accept me back and we could start again. He sounded like he had been drinking and the background noises made me think he was with other people. I politely declined and put the phone down. To him, I hoped I sounded calm and collected but anxiety rose within me. With careful intentionality, we had kept the location of the wedding hidden from him but what if he had found out and turned up? Many different scenarios played out in my mind – none of which had happy endings. I knew he had knives and access to pistols, and possibly the crossbow he had mentioned. Our wedding was to be a family event and ours would not be the only children there. It was hard not to feel intimidated, to keep anxious thoughts in check, to regain a sense of inner peace.

The only thing left to us was prayer. We called our closest friends, and those we knew would pray, and then we prayed ourselves too. It was the only thing we could do but it was also the very best thing to do.

He didn't turn up. By the time people started arriving, the area was soaked in prayer. All through the preparations on site, we asked Father God for clear skies too, even though rain was forecast. He was gracious and kind and the rains held off until the following morning. We had experienced answers to our prayers in very physical ways.

◆◇◆

"Whenever God restores something, he restores it to a place greater than it was before."[14]

Bill Johnson

Our Father God is in the business of restoring broken lives and healing wounded hearts and bodies. It's what living in the Kingdom of God is all about. Moving forward from one degree of freedom to another. My kind new husband is part of my process of restoration. Although not perfect (we are all still on this side of heaven, after all), he is mostly gentle, attentive and kind. He's not particularly physically strong and probably wouldn't win many street fights but he has an inner strength that comes from a certain knowledge of who his heavenly Father is.

When I separated from my first husband, I left behind a five-bedroom house as well as a holiday home on the coast. The lawyer who wrote the divorce agreement said it was the worse financial settlement she had ever penned. This was not important to me. Keeping myself safe was vital. I knew that if I tried to extract unwilling funds from him, I would pay a price. Even if I legally had the right to do so. The cost would be too high. When I was single, it was a struggle financially. Although he would feed the children and pay for their treats and upkeep when they were with him, he never contributed anything financially outside of these times throughout the rest of their childhood years. On one occasion, he strode over confidently into my kitchen, a cheque for a substantial amount in his hand, promising to hand it over to me if I had sex with

14. God's Restoration, Bill Johnson (Bethel Church Podcasts), 2015, https://www.bethel.tv/en/podcasts/sermons/episodes/151

him because I was, after all, still his wife and I had no right to refuse him. At this stage I had taken on a lodger and she was in the kitchen with me. Emboldened, I refused and he stormed off. He never again offered any form of financial assistance.

Be that as it may, my experience is that our Father God is more than able to provide for his children. There was the time when my new husband, myself and four children first moved to the UK. We learned to depend on God for all that we needed. In fact, we once got down to our last £20 with no income in sight. My lovely husband sat on the floor in the corner of our dinning room and cried out to God. That evening, around ten o'clock, he received a call offering him his first job in the UK. We sold a camera to tide us over to the first salary and we were on our way! We have seen our Father provide in so many different ways since then too. We've learned to be content with little and much and hold material things lightly. I've changed from the inside out too. Large houses and expensive possessions have lost their attraction for me. Along the way, my values changed and continue to change.

Physically, I realised that although bruises heal, our bodies have memories. Instinctively, we flinch or twitch and an emotion floods our souls even though no harm was meant. Self-love and patience, as body and soul catch up with a new reality, is needed. Understanding and kindness, patience and tenderness from others helps the restorative process. But it can't be hurried along. Often Father God gives those of us who have been in abusive situations, the gift of just the right people for the stage of healing we are at. These gifts can also come in the form of a book, a course, a dream, an encounter with Jesus, a movie, a chance comment, an opportunity to shine and so much more. Words, gestures, encouragement all contribute.

On a side note, it can be tempting to move from an abusive relationship straight into another relationship – particularly one that seems good and wholesome. It is understandable to do so, especially as we all strongly desire the affirmation and company of others. It's not always wise, however. There is the danger that you will find yourself attracted to someone similar to those you have chosen in the past and this is often particularly true as you leave an abusive relationship. As a broken, hurt and bruised person, you are vulnerable – and, yes, I hated thinking of myself in those terms too! You are also a strong person who has survived against the odds! However, sound advice is to give yourself time to be on your own. To rediscover who you really are and want to be before you start making adjustments within a new relationship to please someone else. It's not about waiting until you're good enough for someone else but rather that you see yourself as Father God sees you – this makes you better able to see others for who they are and then make choices that will benefit you and them.

Apart from the financial and physical restoration, our Father God delights in emotional and spiritual restoration too. My inner being had felt torn, bruised and battered. Bodies heal quicker than hearts and emotions. For all that, hearts and emotions do heal – little by little. Trust in others grows again. Walls come down. Joy becomes part of who we are again. Eventually we are able to comfort others with the comfort that we have experienced. It's an ongoing process – this journey of restoration, of surviving and thriving. It's not just about getting your old self back. We are told that we are becoming more like Jesus, one step at a time. "We can all draw close to him with the veil removed from our faces. And with no veil we all become like mirrors who brightly reflect the glory of the Lord Jesus. We are being transfigured into his very image *as we move from one brighter level of glory to another.* And this glorious transfiguration comes from the Lord, who is the Spirit" (2 Corinthians 3:18, italics added). That is what our

Father God is in the process of doing with us: we're becoming more glorious than we ever were! Day by day. Bit by bit.

Pause and Reflect

I have a question for you – are you expecting restoration? Do you believe Father God can and wants to bring about restoration in your life too? You may not be able to answer that question quickly and confidently. You may have unanswered questions. Things that don't seem to make sense. The most common ones are about God's goodness: How could God let me go through what I've been through? Why didn't he stop it?

I've asked those questions too and I personally don't think there are easy answers. I know we live in a world where Father God has chosen to give each one of us freedom to make choices. I believe God does speak to everyone and some choose to ignore him and do their own thing. If they listened to his promptings, they wouldn't hurt, misuse and abuse others. Those who abuse others do so out of a place of being hurt themselves perhaps. I have heard it said that "hurt people hurt people". I am definitely not making excuses for them – it shouldn't happen.

We live in a world where sin has not yet been eradicated. It's an age of God's grace where there are opportunities for people to turn to him but many choose not to. Even those who do, and my ex-husband was one who professed to being a Christian, can allow their own insecurities and sinful desires to take hold. Being a Christian may start with a decision to be a Christ follower but it continues with daily decisions to remain close to him. Some profess faith but don't live it out.

For me, I felt like Father God was with me through the fire and through the deep waters as he promised: "When you pass through the waters, I will be with you; and when you pass through the rivers, they will not sweep over you. When you walk through the fire, you will not be burned; the flames will not set you ablaze" (Isaiah 43:2). It wasn't easy but I knew he was with me – I would get through.

When it became too much, I ran to Father God and he comforted me, "Praise be to the God and Father of our Lord Jesus Christ, the Father of compassion and *the God of all comfort, who comforts us in all our troubles,* so that we can comfort those in any trouble with the comfort we ourselves receive from God" (2 Corinthians 1:3-4, italics added).

I still had to deal with the disappointment I felt – life had not turned out as I wanted it to – and eventually I did express the anger I felt about this to and at God. It is important to deal with your disappointment and vent that anger (see chapters two and seven).

We are not the first to say there is mystery in all this – I don't understand. Thousands of years ago the psalmist wrote in Psalm 73:16-17, "When *I tried to understand all this, it troubled me deeply* till I entered the sanctuary of God; then I understood their final destiny" (italics added). He saw evil being done and couldn't understand why God wasn't stopping it – until he came before God himself. My experience has been that my heart is settled and my mind stilled when I come into the presence of my loving and good Father God.

My experiences have also helped me to be so much more compassionate, kind and patient than I was. The comfort I received from Father God has meant I have been able to offer comfort to others and point people to the place of his love too. Continuing to grow in the knowledge of his love for me and his goodness in my life, has meant I can open my arms up widely to receive all the ongoing restoration that he has for me! Let me encourage you to do the same!

Know that you are loved, you are treasured, you are a complete delight to our Father God. He wants to fill your life with good things. Not only to restore you to who and what you were, but to give you greater gifts, pour blessings over every aspect of your life, dance with you, feast with you, laugh with you and enjoy being with you. Right now, where you are sitting and reading, take a moment to open your arms as wide as you can and ask our Father God to fill them with good things. Expect to receive. You have a future and a hope.

Appendix

Who We Are

I am redeemed, sanctified and made righteous in Christ
(1 Corinthians 1:30).

I've been transferred out of the kingdom of darkness and
into to the kingdom of God's Son, the kingdom of light
(Colossians 1:13).

All of my sins have been forgiven in Christ (Ephesians 1:7).

I am a new creation in Christ – my old life has passed away
(2 Corinthians 5:17).

God has prepared good works beforehand for me to walk in
(Ephesians 2:10).

I've become the righteousness of God in Christ
(2 Corinthians 5:21).

I can do all things through Christ who strengthens me
(Philippians 4:13).

My God supplies all my needs according to His riches in glory
in Christ (Philippians 4:19).

I am called to be a saint (1 Corinthians 1:2).

I am a child of God (John 1:12, 1 John 3:1-2).

My body is the temple of the Holy Spirit (1 Corinthians 6:19).

It is no longer I who live, but Christ who lives in me
(Galatians 2:20).

God's love has been shed abroad in my heart by the Holy Spirit (Romans 5:5).

Greater is He who is in me than he (Satan) who is in the world (1 John 4:4).

I am blessed with every spiritual blessing in the heavenly places in Christ (Ephesians 1:3).

Because I love God and am called according to His purpose, He is causing all things to work together for good (Romans 8:28).

If God is for me, who can be against me? (Romans 8:31).

Nothing can separate me from Christ's love (Romans 8:35-39).

All things are possible for me because I'm a believer (Mark 9:23).

Because I am His child, God is leading me by His Spirit (Romans 8:14).

God has given me special gifts to use for His service (1 Peter 4:10-11).

I can cast out demons and lay hands on the sick so that they will recover (Mark 16:17-18).

I am an ambassador for Christ (2 Corinthians 5:20).

I have eternal life (John 3:16).

I am the salt of the earth and the light of the world (Matthew 5:13-14).

I am an heir of God and a joint-heir with Jesus Christ (Romans 8:17).

I am a member of the body of Christ (1 Corinthians 12:27).

The Lord is my shepherd, I shall not want (Psalm 23:1).

The Lord is the defence of my life – whom shall I fear? (Psalm 27:1).

God will satisfy me with long life (Psalm 91:16).

Christ bore my sicknesses and carried my pains (Isaiah 53:4-5).

The Lord is my helper, so I will not be afraid (Hebrews 13:6).

I cast all my cares upon the Lord because He cares for me (1 Peter 5:7).

I resist the devil, and he flees from me (James 4:7).

God will complete the good work He has begun in me (Philippians 1:6).

God is at work within me, to do His good pleasure (Philippians 2:13).

Further Reading

Experiencing the Father's Embrace, Jack Frost, 2013, Destiny Image Publishers

Father Heart of God, Floyd McClung, 2007, Kingsway Publications

Mind Renovation: 21 Days of Thought Transformation, Kris White, 2017, Dream Tree Press

Multiplying Disciples: A toolkit for learning to live like Jesus, Phil Wilthew, 2018, Malcolm Down Publishing Ltd

Naturally Supernatural: The Normal Christian Life, Wendy Mann, 2015, Malcolm Down Publishing Ltd

Spiritual Slavery to Spiritual Sonship, Jack Frost, 2013, Destiny Image Publishers

Strengthen Yourself in the Lord, Bill Johnson, 2013, Destiny Image Publishers

Supernatural Ways of Royalty, Kris Vallotton, 2017, Destiny Image Publishers

Sustainable Power, Simon Holley, 2013, Authentic Media

The Hiding Place, Corrie ten Boom, 2004, Hodder & Stoughton

www.refuge.org.uk/get-help-now/recognising-abuse/

www.tsmbedford.org

www.kingsarms.org

www.bethelsozo.org.uk

www.acc-uk.org

www.compassionuk.org

www.one-event.org.uk

www.groundlevel.org.uk

To invite Caroline to speak at your event, please email her at carolinecameron0@gmail.com